insight text guide

Leon Furze

Go, Went, Gone

Jenny Erpenbeck

translated by Susan Bernofsky

First published in 2021

Insight Publications Pty Ltd
3/350 Charman Road
Cheltenham VIC 3192
Australia
Tel: +61 3 8571 4950
Fax: +61 3 8571 0257
Email: books@insightpublications.com.au

www.insightpublications.com.au

A catalogue record for this book is available from the National Library of Australia

Jenny Erpenbeck's Go, Went, Gone / Leon Furze

Leon Furze asserts the moral right to be identified as the author of this work.

ISBNs:
9781922378101 (print)
9781922378118 (digital)
9781922378125 (bundle: print + digital)

Cover design by Gisela Beer
Edited by Fabrice Wilmann
Proofread by Janice Bird

Printed in Australia by Ligare

contents

Character map iv

Overview 1

- About the author 1
- Synopsis 2
- Character summaries 3

Background & context 6

Genre, structure & language 11

Chapter-by-chapter analysis 16

Characters & relationships 37

Themes, ideas & values 47

Different interpretations 57

Questions & answers 62

Sample answer 69

References & reading 72

CHARACTER MAP

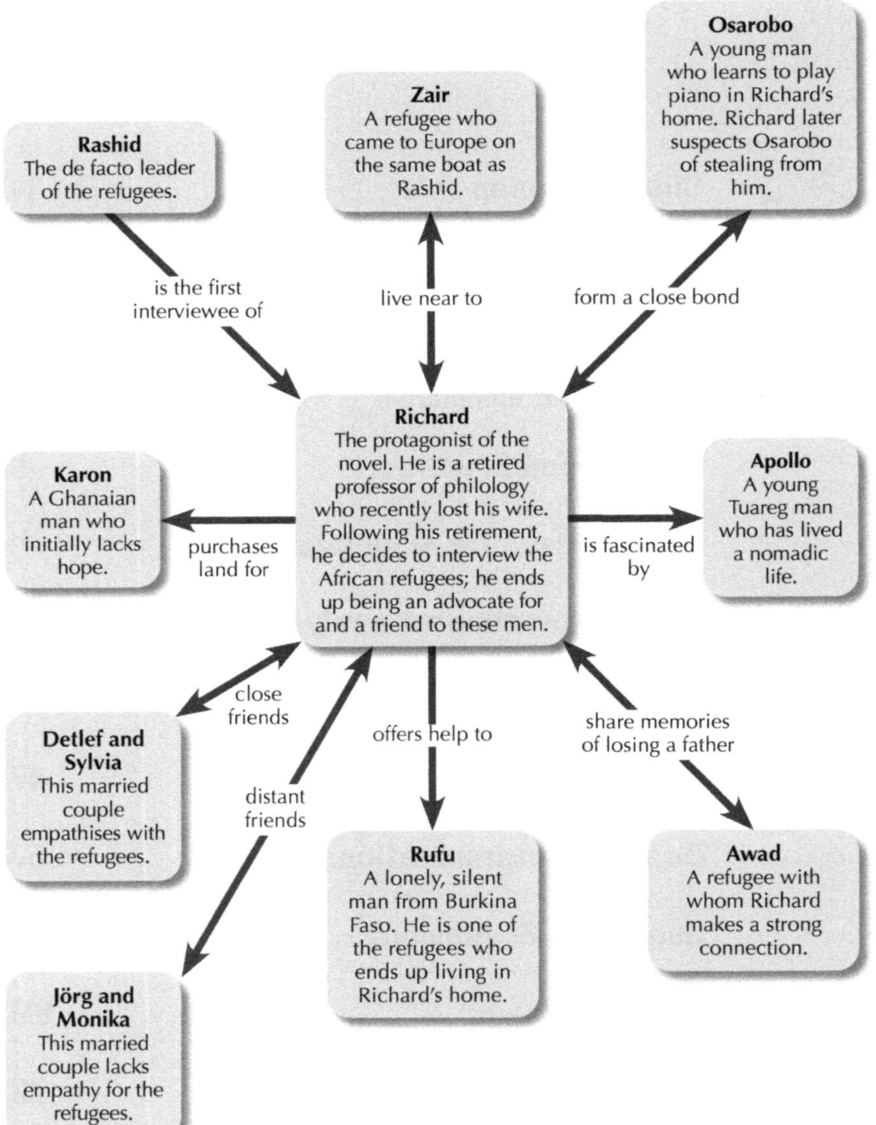

OVERVIEW

About the author

Jenny Erpenbeck was born in 1967 in East Berlin. Her parents were Arabic translator Doris Kilias and physicist, philosopher and writer John Erpenbeck. Jenny Erpenbeck studied theatre at the Humboldt University of Berlin before changing to Music Theatre Director studies at the Hanns Eisler School of Music Berlin. Her interest in music pervades her work, with frequent references to musicians and composers. Erpenbeck started writing in the 1990s, and has written novels, novellas and plays.

Growing up in East Berlin, Erpenbeck experienced firsthand the social and political structures of East Germany. However, she is quick to point out that, aside from the stereotypical perceptions of the German Democratic Republic (GDR), her experience was of a fairly normal, mundane life. In an interview for *The Guardian*, published in 2020 after the release of *Not a Novel: A Memoir in Pieces*, Erpenbeck stated that 'the GDR was also a country with people, with social relations, with a culture, and everyday reality' (Oltermann 2020). This reality is highlighted in *Go, Went, Gone* through the frequent memories and reflections of the protagonist, Richard, about his former life in the East.

Erpenbeck is an experimental but understated writer. Her writing is often poetic, with unusual structures and language choices. Over the course of her writing career she has received many accolades, including the 2015 Independent Foreign Fiction Prize, the 2016 Thomas Mann Prize, the 2017 Strega European Prize and the 2017 Order of Merit of the Federal Republic of Germany. *Go, Went, Gone*, published in German in 2015 and translated into English by American translator Susan Bernofsky in 2017, was listed as a *New York Times* Notable Book and won the Lois Roth Award for translation.

Erpenbeck lives in Berlin with her husband and son. Her works have been translated into over a dozen languages, and she is considered 'one of Germany's finest contemporary writers' (Messud 2017).

Synopsis

Retired professor of German philology, Richard, finds himself adrift following his departure from university life. Richard's wife passed away several years prior to the start of the novel and, now that he has no daily work routine to attend to, he finds himself lonely and bored. While walking through Alexanderplatz in the centre of Berlin, Richard passes – but does not notice – a group of refugee men staging a hunger strike. Seeing the protest later that evening on the news, Richard is surprised that he did not see the men. He becomes interested in their plight and attends an assembly where the men are invited to discuss their issues with the Berlin Senate. The assembly is called to an abrupt halt, but Richard's interest is piqued.

Richard begins researching the men and their African homes. He forms a plan in his mind for a new research project, something to which he can apply his bored academic mind. By the time he decides to interview the men, their tents at Oranienplatz have been torn down and a number of the men have been relocated to a nursing home near where Richard lives. He gains access to the men and begins his interviews, starting with generic questions about their former lives and the reasons they fled their homes. Richard is quickly drawn into the men's lives, learning of horrific stories of war, violence and pain. As he visits the nursing home daily, attending and then teaching German-language lessons, he uncovers the unique histories of the refugees.

Richard's relationship with a number of the refugees deepens: he invites them to his home; acts as an intermediary between them and their lawyers; and involves himself more and more in attempting to untangle the complex legal situation in which they find themselves. After fleeing Africa by boat – a journey that only 550 out of 800 survived

– the men arrived first in Italy. The absurdities of the legal process are continuously highlighted as the men find themselves unable to legally work, first in Italy, then in Germany. The more Richard tries to advocate for the refugees, the more he is confronted by the tangled web of laws and international agreements that essentially mean no European country has to take responsibility for them.

Frustrated and incapable of helping the men to get residency or find work, Richard reaches out in small ways: he invites one refugee into his home to learn piano; he finds volunteer work for another with a friend; he even purchases a block of Ghanaian land for one man's family, so that the man and his relatives can build a life for themselves. As the novel draws to a close, the refugees' unsuccessful asylum applications leave them homeless, and Richard and his friends find space for the men in their own homes. Richard throws a birthday party, a celebration that mixes the cultures of the African refugees and his German friends, and highlights the shared human experience of them all.

Character summaries

Richard

Richard is the protagonist of the novel. A retired professor of philology, he becomes interested in the refugee men's issues. He interviews the men and becomes increasingly involved in their lives.

Rashid (the Olympian / the thunderbolt-hurler)

Rashid is the outspoken informal leader of the refugee group. He lost his children on the voyage from Africa, and his wife subsequently divorced him. He was a metalworker in Africa and is extremely frustrated at his inability to work.

Apollo

Richard names Apollo, one of the first men he encounters, after the Greek god whom Richard believes he resembles. He is a Tuareg man, from the desert. The narrative briefly shifts into Apollo's perspective, making his one of the few voices in the book other than Richard's.

Osarobo

Osarobo is a young man who is interested in learning to play the piano. Richard invites him into his home for lessons and shares his favourite musicians with him. Osarobo is convinced that the Europeans around him think all black men are criminals; Richard suspects Osarobo of burgling his home while he is away at a lecture.

Karon

Karon is first introduced as an unnamed man sweeping the deserted top floor of the nursing home. His actions seem futile, and his story is without hope. After meeting him several times, Richard offers to buy Karon a block of land for his family in Ghana. After the purchase, Karon shares photos of his family with Richard.

Awad (Tristan)

After his father was killed by Gaddafi's men in Tripoli, Awad was forced onto a boat bound for Europe. He feels a deep connection with the other refugees. As it does with Apollo, the text briefly switches to Awad's point of view at one stage.

Rufu

Rufu is a silent, brooding figure who does not mix much with the other refugees. Towards the end of the novel, Richard finds Rufu tranquilised on prescription drugs and helps bring him back to full health.

Detlef and Sylvia

Detlef and Sylvia are Richard's closest friends. Sharing in the grief of Richard's wife's death, they offer Richard a sounding board for his feelings towards the refugees.

Jörg and Monika

Jörg and Monika are a married couple in Richard's circle of German friends. Their attitudes towards the refugees show a lack of empathy and concern, and they frequently make jokes about the refugees and Richard's relationship with them.

BACKGROUND & CONTEXT

The Berlin Wall

Jenny Erpenbeck was born in 1967, six years after the construction of the Berlin Wall. Following the end of World War II in 1945, Germany was divided between the four Allied forces: the United States, the United Kingdom, France and the Soviet Union. Although the city of Berlin was in the middle of Soviet territory, it too was divided between the four powers. Over the next few years, political tensions grew between the Soviet Union and the remaining three Allied powers. France, the US and the UK merged their zones, but the Soviet Union protested against the new policy changes and plans to redevelop postwar Germany.

In 1949, East Germany – the part controlled by the Soviet Union – was declared the German Democratic Republic, or GDR. The Soviets retained their governance over the GDR, and the East continued to diverge from Western Europe, as West Germany developed into a capitalist society alongside the other Allied nations. The East remained communist, and while quality of life began to improve in the West, East Germans increasingly wanted to leave. Throughout the 1950s a great number of people – including some of the youngest, most intellectual members of society – left East Germany for the West. Soviet leader Joseph Stalin met with German officials, and they declared the line between East and West Germany an official border. Barbed wire was erected along the border, but Berlin – still situated in Soviet territory and divided between the Allied and Soviet powers – still allowed some passage between East and West.

In response to the ever-increasing numbers of people leaving East Germany through the 'loophole' of Berlin, police and military personnel in the city closed the border between East and West at midnight on 13 August 1961. Barbed wire fences were reinforced by chain fences, concrete, minefields and armed sentry posts. Overnight, East and West

Germans were separated from one another. Families were split in two, with mothers being separated from their children – even just hours after giving birth, due to the location of the hospitals on either side of the border. The East German government claimed that the wall had been erected to keep out the threat of Western ideologies, but it was clear that the main purpose was to stem the flow of people leaving for the West.

The wall remained for more than twenty years, until 1989. After years of economic decline, the fall of the communist parties of neighbouring countries and consistent pressure from the West, the border between East and West Germany collapsed. In fact, the wall came down largely due to miscommunication. During a press conference on 9 November, it was announced that travel would be permitted between East and West. There was little clarity around the new orders, and people began to turn up at the Berlin checkpoints along the wall. Confused, and with little information from their superiors, the guards were left with no choice but to begin allowing people through. Though initially they followed processes, stamping the passports of those leaving, and even revoking the East German citizenship of some people, eventually the checkpoints were overwhelmed. By nightfall, people were flowing through the checkpoints, while others began dismantling the wall.

Erpenbeck grew up amid this tense and often surreal situation. Her memories of the East – not all of which are negative – infuse her stories. The protagonist of *Go, Went, Gone*, Richard, frequently reminisces on his life before the wall came down. There is even a word for this phenomenon: *ostalgie*, nostalgia for the East. Borders and barriers also suffuse Erpenbeck's writing, and there are reflections on the borders crossed by the African men and those that once encircled Richard.

The African refugee crisis

The United Nations High Commissioner for Refugees (UNHCR) estimates that over 1.3 million people are in need of humanitarian aid in Libya (UNHCR 2017). Due to a complex combination of political unrest, war, and social and economic factors, hundreds of thousands of people have fled the country to seek refuge in other nations since the start of the first Libyan civil war in 2011.

In 2011, forces loyal to Colonel Gaddafi clashed with groups who were aligned with the foreign forces trying to remove him from power. Increasing tension in the country, including violent protests, eventually escalated to a full-blown civil war on 15 February. The United Nations intervened to restrict Gaddafi's access to funds and materials, and also to reduce the likelihood of civilian deaths. However, Gaddafi's forces pushed forward to reclaim major cities along the coast. The ensuing fight led to the bombing and destruction of numerous military and civilian sites. Eventually, Gaddafi was captured and killed on 20 October 2011.

The civil war led to more than a million people fleeing the country or remaining trapped within it and in need of humanitarian aid. Reports coming from the UNHCR indicated that black Africans were being targeted by rebel forces as they tried to flee, and that these people were being subjected to atrocious violations of their human rights. More recently, Amnesty International reported that refugees and migrants from Libya are 'trapped in a vicious cycle of cruelty' (Amnesty International 2020): as they try to flee the horrors of postwar Libya, they are rounded up by international authorities, denied access to European countries and ultimately returned to Libya. Further aspects – such as economic and religious reasons – continue to complicate matters. Corporate interests in oil deposits in Libya mean that certain private companies have a vested interest in who holds power in the country. Some tribes, such as the Tuareg people to whom Erpenbeck's young Apollo belongs, remain loyal to the Gaddafi regime. The situation in Libya continues to worsen, and the cycle of humanitarian abuse shows little sign of resolution.

Seeking asylum in Europe

The distance between Tripoli, in Libya, and the Italian island of Lampedusa is only 300 kilometres, but the journey – over rough seas, in poorly provisioned, barely seaworthy boats – is a harsh one. Boats filled with refugees leave from Libya with the intent of reaching Italian shores. Often, the passengers have paid smugglers for the journey, ending up with hundreds of others in wooden fishing boats. People become sick, some suffocating below decks. Many of the refugees die in transit, and often the ships are wrecked by storm and sea before ever reaching land.

According to a report from Amnesty International, the European Union also actively intercepts vessels at sea and returns them to Libya. The report claims that the EU has been 'collaborating with the Libyan authorities' to provide training and assistance in intercepting the refugees. Upon intercepting the fleeing boats, the migrants are returned to Libya where they are 'subjected to enforced disappearances, indefinite and arbitrary detention, torture and extortion' (Amnesty International 2020).

For the few who survive the journey, the process of seeking refuge and asylum is far from easy. They are detained in detention centres or sent to the mainland for processing. If they are permitted to reside in Italy, they struggle to find work and, if they do, they often earn too little to live on. As the characters in Erpenbeck's novel make clear, life in Italy is only a small step up from the war zones that the refugees are leaving behind. Unable to afford housing, clothing or even food, many continue their journey across Europe, some heading for Germany.

Throughout *Go, Went, Gone*, Erpenbeck refers to laws and regulations that govern the movement and settlement of migrants across Europe. One such law that protagonist Richard studies in detail is 'Dublin II', also known as the Dublin Regulation. According to the UNHCR, the regulation is based on the assumption that all EU member states provide refugees with similar levels of protection. However, as is seen in this novel, the reality is more complex. Asylum legislation varies from country to country, with different governments interpreting the regulations in ways that suit their own needs. The regulation, according to a 2008 review, is 'unfair both to asylum seekers and to certain Member States' (UNHCR 2008).

The European settlement of African refugees is an ongoing issue in a broader humanitarian crisis. A report from the UNHCR's Relief Web in 2019 stated that '13 [EU] States have committed a total of 6169 resettlement places' (UNHCR 2019), but with the millions of people either actively seeking refuge or still trapped by the lasting effects of war, the struggles faced by these people – reflected in the experiences of the characters in *Go, Went, Gone* – are very real.

GENRE, STRUCTURE & LANGUAGE

Genre

Go, Went, Gone is a novel, told in the third person and centred on the protagonist, Richard. Despite being a work of fiction, the issues in the novel are based in reality, and Erpenbeck uses real locations and situations to express her views and values regarding the refugee crisis and the German and European response. Drawing heavily on real laws, regulations and events, the novel is firmly grounded in fact. This makes the stories of the men Richard interviews even more powerful.

Structure

Erpenbeck is an experimental author who often defies novel conventions and breaks from traditional structures. Although the narrative follows a relatively straightforward linear path – beginning, middle and end – the individual chapters often feature unusual structures and techniques.

While most of the novel is written from the third-person limited point of view, locked to Richard's perspective, there are exceptions. In Chapter 13, for example, there is a sudden shift to Apollo's perspective: 'Why should he show a stranger the scars left on his head and arms by beatings given him by his so-called family?' (p.52). This abrupt change in perspective forces the reader to acknowledge the invasiveness of Richard's questions, and also their futility. While Richard asks fairly unimaginative questions about Apollo's family and life in Africa, the refugee is reliving horrific, confronting memories. Similarly, Chapter 27 begins in Awad's perspective, as he details how 'nauseous' he is 'from all the thinking and remembering' (p.131). Erpenbeck uses these brief moments of perspective shift to allow the reader access to thoughts they would not otherwise see.

In an interview for *The Guardian*, Erpenbeck commented on her unusual style for punctuating dialogue:

> I am still shy of quotation marks. They are like frames, but conversations don't take place in picture frames: a conversation includes different layers, not only what's spoken, but also the thoughts underneath, the quick associations. It is always made up of someone talking and someone listening, and I am also interested in the listener. (Oltermann 2020)

These 'different layers' become very clear in scenes such as the dinner party in Chapter 15 (pp.69–71), in which bursts of Richard's friends' conservations and Richard's own thoughts are arranged in a large block of text that covers a range of topics, from holidays and affairs to memories of the GDR.

The style and structure of chapters also varies depending on which character is at the centre of the narrative. For example, chapters involving Karon are often mysterious and sometimes even lyrical, with poetic structures that use repeated phrases such as 'the room was too small' and 'I asked myself: What is wrong with me? I asked myself, and I also asked God' (p.111). Similarly, when the men receive news that they are required to leave Germany, Erpbenbeck repeats the phrase 'has to go' (p.265) after naming and describing each of the men in turn. The phrase 'Where can a person go when he doesn't know where to go?' (pp.266–7) is the only text on each of the next two pages, resembling the free-form structure of poetry.

Intertextuality

As Richard is a philologist – a professor of language and the origin of texts – intertextuality is incredibly important in this novel. Intertextuality includes references to other texts, direct quotes and allusions.

One of the most prominent forms of intertextuality comes from Richard's names for the African men. Richard has 'difficulty remembering the foreign names of the Africans' (p.66), so in his notes he names them after Greek gods and other literary figures. Apollo is named for his resemblance to the Greek god of, among other things, music, poetry and art. Rashid is named *'the Thunderbolt-hurler'* (p.91) after Zeus, the leader of the Gods, for his fiery temper and the way he leads the other refugees. Richard initially labels Awad Tristan, after the hero of the twelfth-century chivalric romance *Tristan and Isolde* and the Wagner opera with whom he shares a similar upbringing.

Throughout the text, Richard relates important events in the men's lives and moments in his journey with them to aspects of literature, particularly that of Ancient Greece, and works of the German playwright and poet Berthold Brecht. For example, when Yussuf proudly exclaims that he 'worked in Italy as a dishwasher', Richard thinks of the Brecht line *'He who laughs has not yet received the terrible news'* (p.124). At another moment in the text, thinking of anti-refugee sentiments being posted online, Richard recalls another Brecht play in which a group of Berliners murder a horse in the streets. Even as it is being 'torn to pieces', the horse feels concern for its murderers, exclaiming *'Help them'* (p.167). Richard contextualises his experiences with the refugees by linking them to what he knows best.

The intertextual references are also often used to highlight the flaws in the laws and regulations surrounding the refugees. In Richard's speech in Frankfurt, he references Seneca: *'Kindly remember that he whom you call your slave sprang from the same stock'* (p.240). He moves through other classics, from Plato, Ovid and Empedocles, all expressing similar messages. Tall Ithemba's lawyer quotes Ancient Roman text that states 'Your own property is in peril when your neighbor's house burns' (p.245) and later, *'It is accounted a sin to turn any man away from your door'* (p.251). These moments serve to highlight the fact that modern German and European laws stand in opposition to millennia-old philosophies on human rights and how we should treat one another.

Symbols

The man in the lake

Richard had planned to go boating regularly on the lake outside his house during his retirement; however, very early on in the novel it is established that a man died there, and his body has not been found (p.5). The man drowned despite there being other people at the lake: they mistook his arm-waving as a joke and rowed away. Richard feels that 'as long as the body of the dead man hasn't been recovered, the lake belongs to him. All summer long ... the lake has belonged to a dead man' (p.10). To make matters worse, the lake is visible from almost every window in Richard's house, making the idea of the drowned man inescapable.

The man in the lake is used as a motif (a recurring symbol) throughout the text. Richard likens the man under the frozen waters of the lake to the memories of Awad's Ghanaian grandmother as she tries to 'fight her way out of the memory-free zone surrounding her grandson' but 'silently sinks back down again' (p.59). The image of the man trapped beneath the frozen lake continues to haunt Richard, who wonders what would happen if he called out to the man through the ice.

In these ways, the drowned man is symbolic of the refugee crisis: he was seen by others as he struggled, but they did not act. Richard cannot escape his view of the lake, just as he can no longer turn away from the plight of the refugees. He feels helpless and powerless in the face of the man's death, just as he does in the face of the laws and regulations that condemn the men he befriends. Finally, it occurs to Richard that 'the lake will forever remain the lake in which someone has died, but it will nonetheless remain forever very beautiful' (p.276) and that he may swim there next summer. In comparison, Rashid wishes to 'cut' out his own memories, and Richard reflects in another water-based metaphor that 'a life ... in which the future refuses to show itself ... is a life without a shoreline' (p.277).

The German language

The novel takes its title from the German irregular verb 'to go' and its various tense forms *'gehen, ging, gegangen'* (p.50). Richard first sees the phrase on a poster in the nursing home. It is repeated on several occasions throughout the novel, including when the men are forced to relocate to a facility in Spandau (p.162).

For the refugees, the German language is symbolic of a new life and new possibilities. Their German lessons in the nursing home, conducted by an Ethiopian woman, are a way for the men to fill time and to better understand the country in which they find themselves. But the language barrier is problematic. Richard converses with the men in German, Italian and English in his interviews, but none of them have a strong enough grasp of these languages to be able to interpret the complex laws that govern their rights to live and work in Germany.

Richard even muses on the inadequacy of the German language in expressing certain thoughts, such as when Awad says 'I don't know where my mind is' (p.64). Richard wonders 'why does German have no word for "mind"?' (p.64), thinking that the rich and complex German language is nonetheless useless for grappling with the complexities of what the refugees face.

CHAPTER-BY-CHAPTER ANALYSIS

Chapter 1 (pp.3–10)

Summary: *Richard is a recently retired university professor and widower. He reflects on his retirement and his new life.*

Erpenbeck immediately establishes a tone of existential angst as she introduces the protagonist of the novel, Richard. He moves from room to room of his house reflecting on his life leading up to his retirement, including the breakdown of his relationship with a former lover, his wife's death, and the retirement that seems to have left him adrift and confused about his role in life. Richard also dwells on the death of a man in the lake near his house, an image that will become a repeated motif throughout the text.

Key vocabulary

Existential: relating to a philosophy of human experience that asks questions about the meaning of life and the purpose of being human.

Q Why do you think Richard's retirement has left him so preoccupied with death?

Chapter 2 (pp.10–15)

Summary: *Richard encounters – but does not really see – the gathering of refugees at Alexanderplatz.*

The chapter begins with a description of a demonstration outside Berlin's Town Hall. Ten refugees gather in Alexanderplatz, silently waiting for a response to their plight from the government. Richard, however, is oblivious. At this point in the narrative, he is characterised as absent-minded and perhaps self-absorbed. Shifting back and forth between Richard's narrative and scenes of a news reporter discussing the demonstration, Erpenbeck illustrates a common response to the refugee crisis: to treat the refugees as invisible.

Key point

Throughout *Go, Went, Gone*, Erpenbeck forces readers to consider their reactions to the refugee crisis. Without being overtly critical, she employs Richard as a reflection of general readers' attitudes. At first, they simply do not see the crisis unfolding in front of them.

Q Is Erpenbeck criticising Richard's actions at this point in the narrative? What makes you think this?

Chapters 3–5 (pp.15–24)

Summary: *Richard sees the Alexanderplatz demonstration on television. Going through the motions of his new daily routine, he begins to learn more about the plight of the refugees from Africa.*

Without the structure of professional life, Richard's days are moored in simple routines such as cooking, buying groceries and, above all else, remembering his past. He frequently reflects on important moments in his life, from times spent with his lover to his family's flight from Silesia (in modern-day Poland) to Germany in his infancy.

The news of the Alexanderplatz demonstration intrudes on his quiet routine, however, forcing him to ask why he did not see the men. Perhaps as a way of distracting himself from the boredom of his new life, Richard turns his academic eye towards Africa, learning the capitals of African countries and perusing the only book of African literature he owns. While searching for more news on the Alexanderplatz demonstration, Richard learns of the refugee encampment at Oranienplatz.

Key vocabulary

Encampment: a place with temporary accommodation, usually consisting of huts or tents.

Q Where does Richard's sudden interest in the African refugees stem from?

Q What does the series of questions in Chapter 5 about the capital cities of African countries suggest about Western attitudes towards Africa?

Chapters 6–7 (pp.25–31)

Summary: *Richard attends an assembly at the refugee-occupied school in Berlin's Kreuzberg district.*

Not entirely sure of the reason for his actions, Richard attends the assembly hosted by the Berlin Senate for locals and refugees at the occupied school in Kreuzberg. Richard's reluctance to identify himself (p.27) speaks both of his reluctance to become involved in the issue and the shame and embarrassment he felt earlier about his ignorance of the problem. The assembly is brought to an abrupt halt and Richard finds himself once again at home, reflecting on his inability to make the 'confession' of revealing his name.

Q Can you think of any other reasons why Richard might have decided not to give his name?

Chapter 8 (pp.31–8)

Summary: *Richard visits Oranienplatz to see more of the refugee encampment. He wanders through the tents and forms an idea to begin a new project.*

Spurred on by his uncomfortable feelings from the night before, Richard decides to visit Oranienplatz during the day to learn more about the refugees. As always, his thoughts are interspersed with reflections on the past, particularly his life in East Berlin before the fall of the Berlin Wall. He weaves his way through refugees and sympathisers, listening to snatches of conversations that reveal some of the issues the men face. As he sits and observes the men around him, he beings to formulate a new project – something to occupy his mind.

Although Richard's involvement in the refugee crisis is still fairly sterile and academic, his unsettling feelings of irritation indicate that he is beginning to become more emotionally invested.

Key point

Until now, it has seemed as though Richard has been moving almost randomly from one thing to the next. His thoughts have been disconnected, and he seems to be struggling with life post-retirement. The refugee crisis gives him something to anchor himself to, and he realises that the idea to do something has been forming in the back of his mind for some time.

Chapters 9–11 (pp.38–44)

Summary: *Richard begins researching and compiling interview questions for the refugees. The tents at Oranienplatz are torn down, and Richard follows the men to a nearby nursing home to begin his interviews.*

At this point it is easy to see how Richard's interrogative, academic mind works. As soon as he has formed the idea for his project, he is spurred into a kind of action not yet seen in the novel. The questions, however, designed to investigate the transition from a normal existence to life as a refugee, still appear naive and shallow. Before Richard can interview any of the men, the camp at Oranienplatz is torn down and the refugees are rehoused. With a newfound sense of purpose, Richard tracks a group of the men down to a nursing home not far from where he lives and uses his academic credentials to access the refugees for his interviews.

Q What differences do you note in Richard's personality compared with what was presented in earlier chapters? What, if anything, has changed?

Q Is Richard's desire to interview the men likely to help the situation?

Chapters 12–13 (pp.44–56)

Summary: *Richard begins his interviews and discovers more about the refugees' journeys from Africa via Italy.*

After being led up to the rooms where the refugee men are living, Richard is introduced to Rashid, Zair, Abdusalam and Ithemba. As Richard begins asking Rashid questions, his narration of the interview is interspersed with the responses from the Nigerian man, creating an unsettling jumble of images that veers back and forth between Richard's inane questions and the horrific details of the boat ride from Africa to Italy. Richard learns how the men are separated in the nursing home by their countries of origin. At the end of his first day of interviews, he vows he will 'listen to everything' (p.48).

When he returns the next day, Richard's thoughts are already becoming increasingly critical of the Berlin Senate. He interviews Apollo, and learns he is from 'the desert' (p.51), coming to the realisation that the straight lines drawn on his Western map possibly have no meaning to the people who live in those countries. The narrative shifts briefly to provide Apollo's perspective, highlighting for a moment the inadequacies of Richard's questions: 'The boy is silent. Why should he tell a stranger that he doesn't know why he never had any parents?' (p.52).

Key point

The majority of the novel is told from a third-person limited point of view and follows Richard's thoughts and actions. However, at times like this, the perspective shifts briefly to another character such as Apollo. Erpenbeck's writing style is unique, and sometimes confusing, but demonstrates the suffering of the refugees in a way that would not be possible if the story was told exclusively from Richard's perspective.

Q What is the relevance of Richard naming the African man Apollo?

Q How might the shift in perspective affect readers' interpretation of events and characters?

Chapter 14 (pp.56–65)

Summary: *Richard returns to the nursing home and interviews Awad, whose story tells of war, loss and hopelessness.*

Returning to the nursing home for the third day in a row, Richard is approached by Awad. At this point, word has spread of Richard's visits and Awad is eager to tell his story. He informs Richard that he has already spoken to a psychologist, and it is clear from Awad's behaviour and excited speech that he has been traumatised by his past. He begins his tale with his mother's death, then moves through a series of seemingly innocuous statements about his work life before telling Richard that his father was shot. He describes to a silent Richard how on the night of his father's death he was rounded up by a military patrol along with hundreds of others before being loaded onto a boat. Awad punctuates his story with comments such as 'war destroys everything' and 'every human being has his few years to live, and then he dies' (p.63). The sense of hopelessness in his words affects Richard deeply. As Awad's story concludes with the reverence he feels towards Oranienplatz – simply for providing a place to sleep and eat – the chapter ends on the poignant reflection 'that there is truly nothing left to say' (p.65).

Q What does Awad mean by the statement 'When you become foreign … you don't have a choice' (p.63)?

Chapter 15 (pp.66–71)

Summary: *Richard reflects on his interviews, questioning the politics and laws surrounding the refugee crisis. He attends a birthday party for his friend.*

As Richard sits at his desk he thinks over the interviews from the past few days, his head filled with questions. He reflects cynically on the 'Dublin II' regulation, which essentially allows European countries to disown the refugees outright. The irony of the refugee crisis is highlighted: the refugees are allowed to leave Italy if they are not granted residency, but no other European country will accept them. Pausing from his work, Richard attends a birthday party for his long-time friend Detlef. The narrative is interspersed with moments of inane chatter, and Richard's attention is split between his current work, his friends and memories of East Berlin before the fall of the wall.

Q How is Richard's attitude towards the African refugees beginning to change?

Chapters 16–17 (pp.72–83)

Summary: *Richard attends a German-language class with the refugees. The following day, he learns of the plan to move the refugees to another facility and attends an assembly held in protest.*

The refugees attend language classes held at the nursing home, run by an Ethiopian woman who had encountered the men at Oranienplatz. She highlights the issues the men face in learning a new language when their heads are already filled with so much disruption. The next day, as Richard arrives to conduct more interviews, he finds the nursing home strangely empty. A guard informs him that the refugees will be moved to a new facility near Buckow and that the men have gathered in the hall used for their German lessons to raise their issues with a member of the Berlin Senate. Richard thinks about the argument between the men and the political representative from the Senate, recalling his own upheaval after the fall of the wall when he 'suddenly found himself a citizen of a different country' (p.81). The matter is settled when a member of the nursing home staff interrupts and informs the assembly that there have been cases of chickenpox reported, meaning that, for now at least, the men cannot be moved.

Q Was Richard's situation – suddenly finding himself a citizen of the Federal Republic of Germany in 1990 – similar to the plight of the refugees? Why or why not?

Chapters 18–19 (pp.84–96)

Summary: *Richard learns about Muslim customs from Rashid. He also tells his friend Sylvia about the refugees.*

As he interviews Rashid, Richard learns of Muslim customs and holidays, and the five pillars of Islam. Throughout the narrative, Richard contextualises what he learns by comparing it to his knowledge of literature. As such, he relates what Rashid tells him about Islam to stories of Jesus and, in turn, to Greek mythology. In the same way, Richard dubs Rashid 'the thunderbolt-hurler' and compares the refugees' travels to *The Travels of Ibn Battuta*. These comparisons are a way for Richard to connect what he sees with what he already knows, in an effort to understand and relate to these men.

The next day, unable to interview the refugees, Richard goes grocery shopping and runs into Sylvia, Detlef's wife. In a brief exchange, the two imagine what it would be like if they found themselves forced to flee for their lives.

Q Erpenbeck weaves the history of Germany – particularly the division of East and West – into the stories about the refugees. How similar are these stories?

Chapter 20 (pp.96–102)

Summary: *Unable to visit the Muslim refugees, who are at prayer, Richard takes a young man named Osarobo to a nearby cafe and learns about his life.*

The moments in the text with Osarobo are particularly poignant, partially due to his young age but also because of the relationship that he and Richard build over the course of the novel. Osarobo is insecure and quiet in Richard's presence. In contrast to most of the novel, Erpenbeck writes a line-by-line dialogue between the two as they sit in a cafe. Osarobo's refrain – 'Life is crazy' (p.99) – seems like an understatement in his story of war, violence and loss. The young refugee bears the scars of war, including an injury to his left eye. And yet, it is Osarobo who challenges Richard's lack of faith, claiming that God saved him and not his friends who died. The chapter ends with Richard promising that Osarobo can visit his home and play his piano.

Q Why is Osarobo's story so compelling?

Q Why do you think Erpenbeck has chosen to write this chapter differently from others, with more dialogue between the characters?

Chapters 21–3 (pp.102–15)

Summary: *Richard spends the weekend reading through the agreement that removed the refugees from Oranienplatz. On Monday, he attends another German class; on Tuesday he resumes his interviews, encountering Karon for the first time.*

Richard sets aside his Sunday for reading through the agreement between the Senate and the refugees; however, once he begins reading it he is shocked by its brevity. He combs through it line by line with a linguist's eye for detail, noting the absurdity of phrases such as '*legally permissible*' (p.103), as if any form of camping in the square would ever be permitted. On Monday, he returns to the nursing home and helps the German teacher to put up posters; she asks him if he would be interested in teaching the more advanced students.

After his interviews on Tuesday, Richard sees a thin man with a broom sweeping the uninhabited second floor. The man's story is hypnotic, written in a series of flashbacks that are recounted to Richard; as Richard recalls them when at home, the sound of the sweeping brush intrudes on his thoughts. Erpenbeck describes these events using language that is almost poetic, with repeated lines and rhetorical questions punctuating the man's story. Lines such as 'I looked in front of me and behind me and saw nothing' (p.115) leave a haunting impression of the plight of the refugees.

Key point

Karon, the as-yet unnamed man in Chapter 23, is another of the refugees with whom Richard builds a close relationship. His manner of speaking and the haunting story he tells are similar to that of Apollo, Rashid and the others, but each man has a unique narrative.

Q What is it about Karon's story that affects Richard so deeply that he cannot get it out of his head when he returns home?

Q What are the similarities and differences between Karon's story and those of the other men?

Chapter 24 (pp.115–23)

Summary: *Richard picks up Osarobo for a piano lesson.*

Richard agrees to pick up Osarobo for a piano lesson. Osarobo appears to have forgotten, and Richard is initially annoyed, then self-critical for not immediately understanding that perhaps for Osarobo the piano is simply a way to pass the time. While waiting for Osarobo, Richard reflects on his former lover and their final arguments, thinking about the fact that his anticipation of their meetings came to outweigh the joy he felt at the meetings themselves. Finally, Osarobo appears and the two walk to Richard's house. Richard asks Osarobo if he has heard of Hitler, then glosses over the atrocities of World War II when he realises that this young man is burdened enough with horrors of his own. The sound of Osarobo playing the piano makes Richard realise that he has been missing something from his life since his wife's death.

Q How does the fact that Osarobo plays piano affect both Richard and the reader?

Chapters 25–7 (pp.123–36)

Summary: *The refugees talk about work. Richard runs into Rufu in the supermarket and invites him to lunch. Awad meets with Richard again, and flees from a blood test for chickenpox.*

In another German-language lesson, the refugees discuss work: what they are qualified for and what they would like to do. In the advanced group, Yussuf proudly declares in perfect German that he is from Mali and worked in Italy as a dishwasher. Richard wryly observes that, although the sentence is perfect, 'as a statement … it spells Yussuf's doom' (p.124) – it marks him out as an unskilled labourer and highlights how unlikely it is that he will gain residency. In reality, Yussuf wishes to be an engineer, and Ali, also in the advanced group, a nurse. Richard thinks of the irony of living in a country with a shortage of skilled workers that refuses entry to refugees seeking work. The lesson ends and Apollo informs the group that the move to Spandau has once again been delayed.

In the supermarket, Richard queues up in front of Rufu. When it is his turn to pay, Richard cannot find his wallet and, for a moment, wonders 'whether Rufu might have … slipped his hand into his pocket' (p.129), the implication being that he stole it. Though Richard states that 'he doesn't want to think that' (p.129), the reality is that his preconceptions of Africans and refugees lead him to question their actions, reflecting the mindset of the general German population. After Rufu pays for his groceries, Richard offers to cook him lunch at his home and invites him to read a copy of Dante's *Divine Comedy* in Italian.

In Chapter 27, the narrative perspective once again shifts to Awad, further highlighting the inadequacies in Richard's interviews. While Richard asks Awad questions about what he packed for the move to Spandau, Awad's mind is filled with images of blood and violence. Confused by the process of giving a blood sample, Awad becomes agitated, panics and flees to his room.

Q Why do you think Erpenbeck has chosen once again to shift the point of view to another character's perspective?

Chapters 28–9 (pp.136–48)

Summary: *Richard tries to find out more about the men's applications for asylum. At home, he reads up on the history of the African nations and discusses the refugees with his friends.*

The staff at the nursing home have little information for Richard on the asylum seekers' applications, and Richard questions the bureaucracy of the process. At home, he reads about the ancestors of the Tuareg – Apollo's people – in Ancient Greek literature from Herodotus. Once again, Richard relies on his skills as a professor of literature to contextualise the African men and their lives. On a walk with his friends Detlef, Sylvia and Thomas, the four of them discuss the modern-day context of the Tuareg people, including the political unrest and exploitation of uranium by the Areva corporation: 'There's more uranium in Niger than nearly anywhere else in the world' (p.146).

Q Richard tries to contextualise the Tuareg people by learning their history – is this a distraction from the modern-day problems these people are facing?

Chapters 30–1 (pp.148–59)

Summary: *Richard and Apollo talk while bailing out Richard's boat. Rufu and Richard travel in Richard's car to a German-language class run for the refugee men.*

Richard is amazed by Apollo's stories of crossing the desert, particularly at how the Tuareg navigate the vast landscape using the stars and their stories. Richard reflects that, as a reader of literature, the connection between words and real, physical space has never been truly clear to him. Even though he knows that works such as the *Odyssey* and the *Iliad* were oral stories before being written, it is not until he hears Apollo speak that he makes the connection.

On Monday, the refugees are scheduled to attend a German-language class outside of the nursing home. As Richard stands among the men, it is clear that he is becoming part of their circle. They trade familiar greetings, and he knows their stories well. Compared to earlier, when Richard could barely remember their names, his relationship with the men has clearly developed. Rufu is not with the other men; Richard goes to find him and then drives him to the language class in his own car. Richard observes the class, helping to record names at the end. He then drives home with Rashid, Rufu and Abdusalam, and the men sing and enjoy each other's company.

Q What is the importance of seeing Richard becoming friends with the refugees?

Chapters 32–4 (pp.160–9)

Summary: *Osarobo visits for another piano lesson. The planned move to Spandau is back on. The men settle into their new temporary home, and on* Totensonntag *(the day on which the dead are honoured) Richard reflects on death.*

Richard collects Osarobo, who got lost on the way to Richard's house, and teaches him to play a C major scale on the piano. The two of them listen to some of Richard's favourite music recordings, and Richard orders two tickets for the *Christmas Oratorio*. On Monday, Richard visits the home to discover that the move to Spandau – delayed due to the chickenpox outbreak – is scheduled for the next day.

Chapter 34 moves quickly through the first few weeks at Spandau: Richard is overwhelmed by the hospitality of the men, such as when Ithemba presents him with an enormous plate of food; Rashid finds unpaid volunteer work for the refugees who are keen to work; and the Foreigners Office begins processing applications. On *Totensonntag*, the day for remembering the dead, Richard reads of the boats capsizing in the Mediterranean. The callous comments in the articles remind him of the anti-Roma and Sinti slogans from twenty-five years ago. Richard visits his parents' graves, ashamed that, for most of his life, he has hoped that 'people from Africa mourn their dead less' (p.169).

Key point

In Chapter 34, Erpenbeck forces us to consider another problematic truth about the refugee crisis. While news articles reduce deaths to statistics – from war, violence or the capsizing of boats between Africa and Europe – every one of these deaths is a real human being with families and friends who mourn them. In the 'luxury' of the family cemetery plot, Richard is deeply ashamed for taking 'the easy way out' (p.169) and ignoring the simple truth that all people grieve.

Q How is death explored in the novel? Is there a difference in how European and African cultures think about death?

Chapters 35–7 (pp.169–75)

Summary: *Advent arrives, and the complications around the asylum applications continue.*

Richard continues visiting the men and inviting Osarobo to his house to play the piano. In talks with Tristan's lawyer, the ongoing absurdity of the laws and regulations surrounding asylum continues. The refugees become more and more disillusioned with the process; Rashid comments that 'they really don't want us here' (p.171). Richard encourages his friend Anne to take on one of the refugees, Ali, to help with her elderly mother.

The men appear stuck in a kind of stasis, and when Richard learns that Osarobo has had to return to Italy to renew his papers, he finds himself wondering if he has given up hope: 'When did he turn from a man filled with great hopes for mankind into an almsgiver? ... Has he now truly relinquished all hope?' (p.175).

Q The pace of the novel seems to be increasing, with time passing in days and weeks rather than one day at a time. Why might Erpenbeck have chosen to do this?

Chapters 38–40 (pp.175–88)

Summary: *Richard considers how the refugees stay connected through their smartphones. The 'iron law' continues to complicate the asylum process. For the first time since his wife's death, Richard decorates his home for Christmas.*

During his first visits to the refugees, Richard had considered their smartphones a 'luxury' (p.179) and wondered how men who were not allowed to work could afford the technology. After spending so long with them, however, he has come to realise that the men rely on the devices to connect with one another, people back home and other communities of refugees around the world. He reflects on the idea that several of the men 'feel more at home in these wireless networks than in any of the countries in which they await their future' (p.177).

Key point

Chapter 39 is largely concerned with the 'iron law' and is interspersed with negative comments towards the refugees from online forums and politicians, such as '*But these cretins … they're all drug dealers or African mafia*' (p.182) and '*Malcontents who've banded together to make trouble*' (p.183).

The law is personified as a beast that will ultimately devour the refugees. The personification of the 'iron law' in this and other chapters adds to the sense of hopelessness around the refugee crisis. As commented earlier in the novel, no one person wrote the laws, and therefore no one person can be blamed. Erpenbeck criticises the lack of empathy shown by those who adhere to the inhumane laws, and the unsettling image of the law devouring 'hand, knee, nose, mouth …' (p.184) seems to mock the idea that the refugees would ever be granted asylum.

Q Why does Erpenbeck choose to personify the law, rather than focus solely on the human politicians, lawyers and judges who enforce it?

Chapter 41 (pp.188–94)

Summary: *Rashid goes to Richard's home for a Christmas meal and tells more of his story.*

Rashid's story is one of the most powerful in the novel: '[Richard] knows that this story Rashid is telling him is something like a gift' (p.191). It comes at a time when Richard has become close friends with many of the refugees and has heard many of their stories. Richard notes the similarities between Rashid's story and the others' – for example, echoing the blood and violence of Tristan's story (p.192). However, it is not the memories of war that have the most profound impact, but instead his recounting of the capsizing of the boat full of refugees off the coast of Italy. The tragedy has been mentioned numerous times in the novel, with the statistic 'approximately 550 of the 800 people drowned' (p.193) finally making a personal impact on Richard when Rashid tells of losing his children.

Interspersed with Rashid's stories of horror and loss are conversations between the men about Rashid's former job as a metalworker. Like the other refugees, Rashid is trapped between his past and the stasis forced on him in the present, unable to work or live freely in any European country.

Q How does Rashid's tragic story help both Richard and readers develop empathy for refugees with similar stories?

Chapters 42–3 (pp.195–206)

Summary: *Osarobo returns after Christmas. Richard offers to buy property in Ghana for Karon's family.*

In the days following Christmas, Richard visits his friends. It is clear that some of his friends, particularly Monika, do not understand the plight of the refugees. Richard visits the men, bringing them birthday presents – as refugees lacking birth certificates and other documents, their birthdays had been recorded by the Italian government as 1 January.

Richard offers to take Karon to court for a police summons and, as they are talking, he learns that a property in Ghana of a size large enough to support Karon's family would be about the price of the riding mower he has been planning to purchase. He offers to buy the land for Karon's family.

Q Is it right of Richard to offer to buy land for Karon's family? Why does he make the offer?

Chapter 44 (pp.206–14)

Summary: *Police arrive to evict the men from the Spandau facility. The refugees protest.*

Chapter 44 offers a tense and climactic moment in the text. After the lull of the previous few chapters, with the men waiting to hear about their applications for asylum, the sudden energy of this chapter is shocking. Richard arrives at the Spandau facility to find twenty police cars circling the building, because the refugees are staging a protest. Richard thinks of the irony that tomorrow's news will probably say the refugees are responsible for the cost of their own removal, 'as used to happen in other periods of German history, with regard to other transports' (p.209). The allusion here is to the transport used to move the Jewish people and others who were targeted by the Nazis, and again the comparison between the refugee crisis and the horrors of World War II is highlighted.

Richard has another moment of realisation in this chapter, acknowledging that 'the difference between one person and another is in fact ridiculously small' (p.210).

Q How has Richard changed from the beginning of the text, when he did not even notice the men protesting at Alexanderplatz, to now?

Chapters 45–7 (pp.214–28)

Summary: *The men march. Another group of refugees holds a protest on the roof of their residence. Richard purchases land for Karon's family.*

Following the eviction from Spandau, the men march from Oranienplatz to the Berlin Senate in protest. The march is held up by more ridiculous bureaucracy. Richard applies for the permit to allow the demonstration to occur and even devises the slogan: '*A Time to Make Friends*' (p.215). Although he initially marches with the men, after they reach Moritzplatz 'he goes down into the subway and returns home' (p.217).

That evening, Richard watches another protest on the news: refugees have occupied the roof of their residence and are refusing to move. Online slander against the refugees continues, and one newspaper claims that the refugees are the victims of 'sympathizers, being used as tools to serve others' political goals' (p.221). Richard is interrupted by a message from Karon, who has an appointment with the district authorities. Over the next few days, Karon arranges the purchase of a block of land in Ghana.

Q Does it seem as if the refugees' protests will be effective? Why or why not?

Q Why do you think Richard leaves the demonstration early?

Chapters 48–51 (pp.228–51)

Summary: *Richard helps Rufu, and Osarobo resumes his piano lessons. Richard receives an invitation to participate in a colloquium; as he is planning his speech, he learns that the refugees are being challenged by the law once again. He visits Ithemba's lawyer.*

Richard spots Rufu near the Friedrichshain residence where refugees are occupying the roof in protest. Rufu is clearly unwell, and he reveals to Richard that he has been taking medication. Richard's friends inform him that the pills are strong sedatives with a host of side effects. When Richard reads through the list of side effects online, he suddenly recalls a Bach cantata: 'Slumber now, ye eyes so weary, / Fall in soft and calm repose! / World, I dwell no longer here, / Since I have no share in thee / Which my soul could offer comfort' (p.231). Again, Richard is using his cultural knowledge to understand the world around him. He takes Rufu to a dentist, where they discover that a cavity has been the cause of his pain all along: 'Rufu had spent Christmas confined to a psychiatric ward of a Berlin hospital and ... was prescribed medication that ... nearly killed him, and now it turns out the reason for all of this may have been just a hole in a tooth' (p.235).

Osarobo, meanwhile, has been living with a man from the Ivory Coast. Richard invites Osarobo over for more piano lessons, learning that he must return to Italy in eight weeks for his papers.

Planning his speech for the colloquium, Richard's attention is constantly drawn to passages from texts in which the similarity between all people is highlighted. As he is drafting his paper, he learns that the Berlin Senate has retroactively declared the agreement with the refugees invalid. Ithemba's lawyer reveals even more complicated and ridiculous laws that the refugees face, such as their inability to work even if they were permitted to stay, due to the preferential employment of Europeans.

Key vocabulary

Colloquium: an academic conference or seminar.

Q What do Richard's selections of texts for his speech reveal about how his world view has changed since the start of the novel?

Q How does the lack of understanding of the language, culture and norms of German society adversely affect refugees such as Rufu?

Chapters 52–3 (pp.251–64)

Summary: *Richard speaks at the colloquium. He returns home to find he has been burgled and suspects Osarobo of committing the crime. Karon visits Richard's house.*

After a moderately successful talk at the colloquium, Richard returns home to find his house has been burgled. Instantly, his suspicions turn towards Osarobo, who knew he was leaving for Frankfurt. Feeling both guilty at his suspicions and upset at the possibility, Richard tries to contact Osarobo. To make matters worse, Osarobo cancels his meetings with Richard and appears to be avoiding him. Richard finds himself overwhelmed and weeps like he has not since his wife died. Karon arrives suddenly, and he and Richard look at photos of Karon's family and the new property.

Q Why does his suspicion of Osarobo upset Richard so much?

Chapter 54 (pp.264–75)

Summary: *The remaining men receive news of their applications. Richard joins efforts to give the men temporary homes.*

After the review of individual cases, it is decided that the responsibility for the refugees is borne by Italy. Erpenbeck lists the refugees one at a time, repeating that each man 'has to go' (p.265). The phrase 'Where can a person go when he doesn't know where to go?' (pp.266–7) is repeated on two individual pages, standing out against the rest of the novel. The remainder of the chapter is devoted to describing where the men will stay now that they have been officially evicted. Richard offers up his home to a number of the refugees and encourages his friends to do the same. The men carry out odd jobs and attend meetings, and Abdusalam cooks for them.

Key point

In the face of the 'iron law', it appears that the refugees have finally lost. They are now required to leave for Italy, where they will once again be sucked into that country's bureaucratic processes. Faced with the men's eviction, and having built strong relationships with them, Richard offers up his own home. Even so, with all their efforts only 147 of the 476 men are rehoused, and 'Richard doesn't know what has become of the 329 others' (p.272).

Q Why does Erpenbeck single out the question 'Where can a person go when he doesn't know where to go?' in this chapter?

Chapter 55 (pp.276–83)

Summary: *Richard organises a birthday party. The refugees and Richard's friends share their stories.*

Richard has not held a birthday party since his wife's death. Now, he organises a large party, inviting the refugees and his German friends. They prepare meals, both German and African, and clear Richard's garden for the party. Sylvia's illness, and the toll it is taking on her husband Detlef, becomes a point that unites a number of the men. They sit around the fire and reflect on the 'women they have loved, who once loved them' (p.279). Karon, Rashid, Tristan, Khalil, Ithemba and Apollo talk about their experiences of love.

Finally, Richard reveals the shame and fear that surrounded his late wife's abortion, which he had talked her into having. The novel ends on a poignant note, with Richard acknowledging 'that the things I can endure are only just the surface of what I can't possibly endure … like the surface of the sea' (p.283).

Q Why does Richard choose this moment to share the secret of his wife's abortion?

Q Does the novel end with a sense of hope or hopelessness?

CHARACTERS & RELATIONSHIPS

Richard

Key quotes

'Why is it that Richard ... doesn't hear this silence?' (p.11)

'No, Richard doesn't want to say his name.' (p.27)

'Richard is having difficulty remembering the foreign names of the Africans, so when he sits at his desk taking notes in the evening, he transforms Awad into *Tristan*, and the boy from the day before yesterday into *Apollo*.' (p.66)

'When did [Richard] turn from a man filled with great hopes for mankind into an almsgiver? ... Has he now truly relinquished all hope?' (p.175)

'I think that's when I realized, says Richard, that the things I can endure are only just the surface of what I can't possibly endure.' (p.283)

Richard, a recently retired professor and widower, is the protagonist of the novel. At the outset of *Go, Went, Gone*, he is adrift, unsure of his purpose and simply going through the motions of his new daily routines. He spends a great deal of his time reminiscing about his past, sometimes with nostalgia, sometimes with regret. In particular, he thinks a lot about the broken relationship with his wife, and the love affair that was one of the causes of his marital problems.

Richard was a professor of philology: the study of classic literature. This gives him another predisposition towards the past, as he often finds himself returning to classics in order to understand the present. Bored and listless in his newly retired life, he latches on to the story of the refugees for the academic challenge of understanding their plight. However, at first Richard does not even notice the men protesting at Alexanderplatz. Reflecting the casual disregard for refugees common in society, he walks right by a protest, and only later when he views it on television does he become concerned.

Once he is involved, however, Richard quickly forms relationships with the men whom he interviews. He decides to make sense of 'how one makes the transition from a full, readily comprehensible existence to the life of a refugee' (p.39). He likens the refugee men to characters from his much-loved classics, such as Tristan, Zeus and Apollo, and sees in them the same heroic and human traits bestowed to people in literature. Over the course of the novel, Richard gains more and more understanding of the hopelessness of the refugees' situations and learns, to his horror, how much his own country's government and laws are complicit.

Richard tries to grapple with the 'iron law' (p.180): he helps the refugees to navigate their asylum applications; he mediates between them and lawyers; and, ultimately, he invites them to live with him when they are exiled from their state-sanctioned homes.

Through his relationship with the men, Richard learns to come to terms with some of the problems in his own past, including the abortion he encouraged his wife to have and the breakdown of his marriage. Richard's character progresses from a rather conceited, self-absorbed academic to a much more humane and understanding man who has profound feelings of empathy for the African men.

Rashid (the Olympian / the thunderbolt-hurler)

Key quotes

'Rashid, and Zair ... were in the same boat ... When the Italian coast guard tried to take the refugees aboard, all of them rushed to one side of the boat, and that's why the boat capsized ... 550 out of 800 drowned.' (p.47)

'*For a hard foe is the Olympian to meet in strife* ... Without even noticing Richard, Rashid thunders down the stairs.' (p.77)

'Rashid is shouting that he's had enough, he's going to set everything on fire, tear down the building, blow it all up, smash the furniture, tear off the roof, kick down the doors ...' (p.211)

Rashid is the first man to be interviewed by Richard, and acts as a de facto leader of the group of refugee men. He introduces Richard to the other Africans, and Richard quickly learns that Rashid arrived in Europe after a disastrous sea voyage in which over half of the people crammed into the crowded boat drowned. Richard dubs Rashid 'the thunderbolt-hurler' after he sees him springing into action to protest the planned rehousing of the refugee men from the nursing home. His personality is forthright and occasionally threatening, like his Olympian namesake.

When the men are moved to a refugee complex in Spandau, however, Rashid shows a gentler side. His natural tendencies towards leadership result in him finding unpaid work for his fellow refugees, and he tells Richard 'we're glad when we have something to do' (p.165).

At Christmas, Rashid reveals to Richard more of the horrors of his journey. He tells him of his former life as a metalworker, and how his family moved from Kaduna, Nigeria to Tripoli, Libya (p.190). Once there, the routine of his family's life was overturned the day the soldiers came. Rashid and his children, three-year-old son Ahmed and five-year-old daughter Amina, were taken by the soldiers to a camp and then loaded onto a boat with around 800 people. During the horrific journey, equipment broke, food and water ran out, and finally the motor gave up. After the boat capsized, Rashid, who was able to hold on to a cable, watched the corpses of others on the boat – including his own children – float in the water around him.

It is little wonder then that Rashid is prone to moments of violent rage, such as when the men find that they are to be evicted again from the Spandau complex. In a climactic moment, Rashid rails against the 'column of forty police officers in their military costumes' (p.211) who have come to escort the men away.

Like the other men, Rashid gives Richard – and the reader – insight into the plight of the refugees. The men have all fled persecution in Africa for different reasons, whether due to religious conflict or the fallout from the Gaddafi regime. Rashid's candid and powerful story creates empathy with men who are otherwise reduced to a statistic, such as merely one of the '550 out of 800' (p.47) who drowned.

Apollo

Key quotes

'Why should he show a stranger the scars left on his head and arms by beatings given him by his so-called family?' (Apollo, p.52)

'If I have to go, I can go, Apollo says. I don't have a family to support. I'm free. In Italy I lived on the street for six months once.' (p.170)

A member of the Tuareg people, a nomadic Berber ethnic tribe, Apollo 'looks exactly the way Richard always imagined the Greek god Apollo would look' (p.51). The young man is another of Richard's first interviewees, and Erpenbeck gives rare insight directly into his thoughts. Apollo tells Richard – possibly jokingly – that he is *'del deserto'* (p.51), of the desert. But when Richard begins his interview questions, the narrative perspective shifts to the point of view of Apollo, who wonders 'why should he tell a stranger that he doesn't know why he never had any parents' and reveals that his so-called family 'tried to beat him to death' (p.52).

Through his conversations with Apollo, particularly those about the way in which Tuareg people navigate the desert using only their memories, Richard comes to the conclusion that 'without memory, man is nothing more than a bit of flesh on the planet's surface' (p.151). Apollo is sparing with his information. Unlike other men, such as Rashid and Awad, he does not open up entirely to Richard. However, the interactions with him are just as vital in opening Richard's eyes to the crisis faced by the refugees.

Osarobo

Key quotes

'Exert himself as he will, Osarobo is unable to put an end to his own exertions.' (p.122)

'The soul of Osarobo … is now flying out into the universe, flying somewhere where there are no longer any rules, where you don't have to take anyone else into consideration, but in return you are left forever, completely and irrevocably alone.' (p.261)

When Richard meets him, Osarobo is a quiet, reserved young man who seems uncomfortable in his own skin. He plucks at his hands while talking with Richard, possibly a nervous tic that Richard reads as him being unable to 'put an end to his own exertions' (p.122).

Like some of the other refugees, Osarobo seems despairing, even hopeless. Learning that Osarobo would like to play the piano, Richard invites him to his house and offers him lessons. But the young man still seems distant and forlorn. He comments to Richard that, when he was in Italy, people would move away from him on public transport. He is worried that Europeans believe all black men are criminals.

Later, ironically, Richard is burgled and Osarobo appears a likely suspect. Richard had told him he was going away to deliver a speech at a conference, and after the robbery Osarobo avoids Richard's calls and messages, and the two do not meet again. Richard thinks that, even if Osarobo did rob him, it is more an indication of the desperate place Osarobo resides in than a true reflection of his character. Still, the idea of him being responsible brings Richard to tears.

Osarobo represents some of the negative stereotypes of African refugees that the right-wing press in Germany are all too happy to focus on. Throughout the novel, Richard reads articles in print and online about the refugees and their laziness, their unwillingness to work and the negative impact their presence will have on German society. The hopelessness that Osarobo feels – whether he is indeed responsible for the crime or not – is indicative of a wider sense of futility shared by the refugees in the face of a country that seemingly does not want them.

Karon

Key quotes

'I look in front of me and behind me and I see nothing.' (Karon, p.108)

'The problem is very big, Karon says. I have no wife and no children, he says – I am small. But the problem is very big, it has a wife and many, many children.' (p.203)

'Here in this place, Karon knows his way around, and for a moment he's no longer a refugee, he's a man like any other.' (p.226)

'Karon sends a text ... *always Good morning* ... Always good morning, Richard thinks, indeed what better thing to wish a friend?' (p.228)

When Richard first encounters Karon he is an unnamed and elusive character. He appears on the stairwell of the nursing home where the refugee men stay after Oranienplatz, sweeping dirt from one step to another and back again. His movements are hypnotic, and Richard's thoughts later that evening are confused with snatches of their conversation.

Karon's speech is almost poetic and filled with despair. In that first meeting, he tells Richard, 'I look in front of me and behind me and I see nothing' (p.108). Later, once Richard has learned Karon's name and spent more time with him, he learns of Karon's family at home in Ghana. Feeling increasingly impotent in his abilities to help the refugees, Richard decides to buy a plot of land in Ghana for Karon's family. The gesture is extravagant, but realistically the land costs Richard the same as a small holiday or a new luxury item for his own home.

Karon's gratitude towards Richard is expressed simply: he sends him a photograph of the deed of sale and wishes him 'always Good morning' (p.228). Later, Karon shares photographs of his family with Richard. Although Karon's story begins with a sense of utter hopelessness, Richard is able to offer at least this one refugee some comfort and hope.

Awad (Tristan)

Key quotes

'Awad opens the door wider to invite [Richard] in, he'd like to tell him his story … Because if you want to arrive somewhere, you can't hide anything.' (p.57)

'War destroys everything, Awad says.' (p.63)

'Isn't it like this, Awad says: every adult human being – man or woman, rich or poor, if he has work or not, if he lives in a house or is homeless, it doesn't matter – every human being has his few years to live, and then he dies?' (p.63)

In Richard's first interview with Awad, the man makes it clear that he has already told everything of note to the psychologist. He is animated and agitated, but he nevertheless tells Richard his entire story. Richard learns of Awad's early life in Ghana and that he moved to Libya with his father at the age of seven. Awad speaks highly of his father and reminds Richard of his relationship with his own father. However, during the unrest in Libya, Awad's father was killed by Gaddafi's men. Awad – who Richard refers to as Tristan in reference to the classic text *Tristan and Isolde* – was forced onto a boat with hundreds of others. They were threatened with being shot if they tried to flee, and thus Tristan was compelled to make the journey by sea to Italy. Many of the people he shared the boat with died en route.

Awad also tells Richard of the hardships he has faced since arriving, first in Italy, then in Germany. In a moment similar to the perspective shift to Apollo's point of view, Erpenbeck also grants readers access to Awad's thoughts later in the text. While Richard asks inane questions about the contents of Awad's luggage, the man thinks about 'beatings and bullets' and notes that 'the thinking is lodged in his head like a shattered animal' (p.132). Like the stories of the other refugee men, Awad's revelations add a human element to the otherwise faceless refugee crisis.

Rufu

Key quotes

'Rufu comes to the front, as an example of someone who is always alone' (p.126)

'Like an old man, Rufu cautiously places one foot before the other to move forward, supporting himself by leaning on Richard, who's linked arms with him … Richard brings him back to the bench, this old man who's only twenty-four.' (p.230)

Rufu is another of the refugees, from Burkina Faso. He is a silent and lonely man who generally keeps his distance from the other refugees and speaks very little. Richard encounters him on a number of occasions, including during the language classes to which the men are signed up. On one occasion, Rufu helps Richard by paying for his groceries when Richard cannot find his wallet. In return, Richard cooks for Rufu and lends him a copy of Dante's *Divine Comedy* in Italian.

Towards the end of the novel, after the escalating protests and during the hunger strike by a number of refugees on the roof of their apartment building, Richard finds Rufu outside alone, tranquilised on prescription drugs. He takes Rufu home and encourages him to stop taking the drugs. Ultimately, he discovers that the source of Rufu's pain is a simple dental cavity, and Richard's dentist deals with it for free. Rufu is one of the men who ends up moving into Richard's house after the men are evicted from Spandau.

Rufu is another character who demonstrates both the complexities and hopelessness of the refugee crisis, and the power of the small acts of kindness people such as Richard can carry out.

Detlef and Sylvia, Jörg and Monika

Key quotes

'Sylvia, his friend's second wife, is a quiet one. You can tell just by looking that she hasn't had an easy year.' (Richard, p.70)

'What does "freedom of movement" mean if not the right to travel?' (Monika, p.197)

'It's a refugee. I understand ... these guys still believe in the medicine man. You dance around him in a circle a few times, and he'll be as good as new.' (Jörg, p.232)

Detlef is Richard's closest friend. Their circle of friends is small but companionable, with even Detlef's first wife, Marion, still coming to their parties and dinners. Detlef's second wife, Sylvia, is also a good friend of Richard's. Sylvia has been ill for a year, and Detlef mentions at the end of the novel that her recent medical examinations did not go well. Detlef and Sylvia are compassionate and understand Richard's relationship with the refugees, even agreeing to house some of the men when they are evicted from Spandau.

Monika and Jörg, on the other hand, represent the shallow and callous side of public opinion towards the refugees. They make crass jokes about African women having diseases, and Jörg quips that Africans still believe in 'the medicine man' (p.232) when Richard contacts him for advice about Rufu's medication. Monika's comment that freedom of movement means the 'right to travel' (p.197) is ironic given the circumstances: she is talking of holidays, while the refugees are essentially trapped by laws and regulations governing their freedom. It is telling that, at the end of the novel, Monika and Jörg are not invited to Richard's birthday party.

Richard's circle of friends represents how the idea of hardship varies from person to person. Richard believes that he has suffered hardships, including the death of his wife. Yet at a dinner party with his friends he finds himself tuning out the inane chatter and complaints of his associates, and when he reflects on his own life in comparison with the refugees' he realises that he has known very little suffering. At Richard's birthday party though, both the Germans and the Africans share a moment of grief when Detlef talks about Sylvia's illness, once again demonstrating that there are more similarities between these people than differences.

THEMES, IDEAS & VALUES

The refugee crisis

Key quotes

'The sign ... on which black letters spell out in English: *We become visible*.' (p.14)

'When an entire world you don't know crashes down on you, how do you start sorting it all out?' (p.48)

'[I]n wartime there's nothing but beatings and bullets, beatings and bullets ...' (Awad, p.132)

'The practical thing about a law is that no one person made it, so no one is personally responsible for it.' (p.218)

Despite its fictional status, *Go, Went, Gone* is deeply informed by the real-life refugee crisis in Africa. During the horrific reign of Colonel Gaddafi, the authoritarian leader of Libya, hundreds of thousands of people fled the country. The text focuses on several refugees, primarily those who left Libya by boat, arriving first in Italy and later in Germany.

At the outset of the novel, it is unclear what the refugees want. The reader is placed in a position of ignorance, and the refugees themselves 'are silent' (p.11). However, theirs is a deliberate silence, and Erpenbeck uses the 'silence of these men who would rather die than reveal their identity' (p.11) to identify the first issue with the refugee crisis: visibility and accountability. Richard walks through Alexanderplatz but is oblivious to the men's protests. He represents the vast majority of people who are oblivious to the plight of the refugees. There is an irony in the fact that, while in Alexanderplatz, Richard passes a sign reading '*We become visible*' (p.14), but it is not until later that he sees the protest on the news and wonders, 'why didn't [he] see these men at Alexanderplatz?' (p.19).

When Richard finally begins to 'see' the refugees, his academic interest in their plight takes over the narrative. He decides to interview the refugees who have 'been locked up' in time (p.38) and are camping out in

Oranienplatz with no legal residency status or rights to work. He wonders about 'how one makes the transition from a full, readily comprehensible existence to the life of a refugee' (p.39), but his academic interest quickly becomes personal as his interviews progress. Erpenbeck demonstrates that most of us, like Richard, only have a vague understanding of the refugee crisis; at best, it is usually an academic interest in the facts and figures that we can see on the news. However, it is the personal lives of the individuals that begin to change Richard's outlook.

This shift towards a more humane interest is evident from early on, when, exhausted by the lengthy interviews, Richard thinks, 'When an entire world you don't know crashes down on you, how do you start sorting it all out?' (p.48). Richard – and the reader – becomes increasingly aware of the situation faced by the refugees through comments from the men, as when Tristan states, 'When you're foreign, you don't have a choice anymore' (p.80). Through stories such as Awad's, we learn that the reality of war is 'nothing but beatings and bullets, beatings and bullets' (p.132). The sense of hopelessness felt by the men is exacerbated by frustrating laws and regulations of 'a country that suffers from a shortage of trained workers but is nonetheless unwilling to accept these dark-skinned refugees' (p.125). Throughout the text, Erpenbeck is highly critical of German and European refugee and asylum laws, such as 'Dublin II', that restrict the human rights of the refugees.

Though the laws and regulations are cold and sterile, it is their human impact that Erpenbeck focuses on. The 'iron law' (p.180) is personified as an unfeeling beast that 'opens its mouth up terrifyingly wide' (p.183) and devours the refugees 'hand, knee, nose, mouth, feet, eyes, brain, ribs, heart, or teeth' (p.184). In a poignant moment of reflection, thinking of the stories of Rashid and Awad, Richard comes to the cynical conclusion that 'a murdered father and two drowned children are nothing compared with a degree in Economics and Social Sciences' and that 'the practical thing about a law is that no one person made it, so no one is personally responsible for it' (p.218).

Through the heartbreaking, deeply personal stories of the refugees, Erpenbeck criticises those who would value economic expediency and the law over human rights and lives.

Changing perspectives

Key quotes

'Why is it that Richard ... doesn't hear this silence?' (p.11)

'[Richard] is reminded that one person's vantage point is just as valid as another's, and in seeing, there is no right, no wrong.' (p.55)

'For much of [Richard's] life, he's hoped in a tiny back corner of his soul that people from Africa mourn their dead less ... Now, this back corner of his soul is occupied instead by shame: shame that for most of his lifetime he's taken the easy way out.' (p.169)

'I think that's when I realized, says Richard, that the things I can endure are only just the surface of what I can't possibly endure.' (p.283)

Over the course of *Go, Went, Gone*, Richard's perspective on the refugee crisis, as well as his connection with the men he interviews, changes dramatically. Moving from total obliviousness to a deeply personal association, Richard's viewpoint on the issue evolves to become much more empathetic. However, it is not just his perspective on the refugee crisis that develops through this process, but also his understanding of himself.

Richard's perspective on the world begins to change from very early on in his interviews. In one of his first conversations with Apollo, in which a comparison is drawn between life in the desert and the temporary Oranienplatz camp, Richard recalls learning how dust from Africa travels in the air across to Europe. In that moment, he 'is reminded that one person's vantage point is just as valid as another's' (p.55). With each interview, he learns more about the lives of the African men, highlighting gaps in his own knowledge and understanding of the world. Rather than recoiling from his shortcomings, however, he takes the opportunity to learn more, studying the geography of Africa, as well as the language, literature and history of its countries. Through Richard, Erpenbeck demonstrates the importance of being open to changes in perspective.

A turning point occurs towards the latter half of the novel. Richard, who once had 'difficulty remembering the foreign names of the Africans' (p.66), stands among the men, exchanging amicable greetings and recognising them by their faces, belongings and stories (p.153). At this point in the novel, Richard also undergoes a moment of self-realisation. During *Totensonntag*, the day of remembrance for the dead, he realises that 'for much of his life, he's hoped in a tiny back corner of his soul that people from Africa mourn their dead less' (p.169). The thought of this fills him with 'shame that for most of his lifetime he's taken the easy way out' (p.169). As his relationships with the men develop, so too does Richard's own humanity.

His growing understanding of the legal situation of the refugees also prompts a shift in his perspective towards the politics of his own country. When the men protest their eviction from Spandau, Richard observes that 'a border ... can suddenly become visible' (p.209). This metaphorical border reminds him of a story of a mythical line dividing two halves of the universe, and he questions whether it is also 'a rift between Black and White ... Poor and Rich ... those whose fathers have died and those whose fathers are still alive' (p.209). The list of comparisons goes on, and Richard finally comes to the conclusion that 'the difference between one person and another is in fact ridiculously small' (p.210). The scene ends with the ironic observation that people in Berlin – once surrounded by a physical wall – have forgotten that 'a border isn't just measured by an opponent's stature but in fact creates him' (p.211). The borders that separate the refugees and the Germans, Richard has come to understand, only exist in people's minds.

The shared humanity of the refugees and the Germans is exemplified in one of the final scenes in the novel. Throughout the text there has been an obvious difference between Richard's life of comfort and the struggles of the refugee men. At Richard's birthday party, however, it is clear that all of the men – whether African or German – share certain perspectives. As the men sit and 'think for a moment about women they have loved, who once loved them' (p.279), it is clear that they share these perspectives of love and loss. Driven by these shared experiences, Richard reveals a part of himself he has never shown before. He talks about his wife's abortion, carried out at his insistence, and the rift that opened between them. Thinking of his wife's death, Richard says, 'I think that's when I realized ... that the things I can endure are only just the surface of what I can't possibly endure' (p.283).

Through the relationships he develops with the refugee men, Richard experiences a shift in his perspectives on his country, the world and his own life.

The meaning of life

Key quotes

'Hope is what's keeping them alive, and hope is cheap.' (p.104)

'I look in front of me and behind me and I see nothing.' (Karon, p.108)

'The line dividing ghosts and people has always seemed to [Richard] thin ...' (p.222)

In many ways, Richard's journey throughout *Go, Went, Gone* is an existential one – concerned with questions about the meaning and purpose of his own life, and of life in general. Through his interviews and developing relationship with the refugees, he comes to understand that the world around him is bigger than he had imagined, and his place in it different from his expectations.

Richard's thoughts are preoccupied with life and death from early on in the novel – a natural consequence of his recent retirement. He wonders whether he has 'many more years ... or perhaps only a few' left before him (p.3), and he spends his time in the opening chapter ruminating on the 'invisible link' (p.9) that will connect his belongings to the various people who will inherit them after his death. Coupled with the recurring image of the dead man in the lake, these morbid thoughts may seem self-pitying, but Richard's loneliness after his wife's death and his retirement means that the idea of death is always close at hand.

Richard's cynicism also colours his world view. Reflecting on the different layers of history that make up the world around him, Richard considers that 'the earth is more like a garbage heap ... and progress is only when the creatures walking the earth know nothing of all these things' (pp.20–1), an image repeated in the excerpt he reads from *Negerliteratur*: '*Under the earth there is only more earth. What comes after that, no one knows*' (p.24). Richard finds it hard to see beyond the arbitrary boundaries that separate layers of history, language and meaning, often finding himself dredging up memories of the past from before the collapse of the wall or relying on his knowledge of ancient literature to understand the world around him. He questions these boundaries, asking 'what makes a surface a surface?' (p.31). In the earlier parts of the novel, Richard relies on his intellect and memories to form his understanding of the world, but, as the novel progresses, he learns that this is not enough.

When Richard first encounters the refugees, it is as an academic exercise: intellectual stimulation to fill the void in his life after retirement. However, after spending some time with the refugees, Richard begins to understand that perhaps his problems are not as great as he had thought. The lack of hope presented by some of the men who 'can't afford a lawyer' and 'barely understand German' (p.104) spurs Richard into action. Through powerful moments, such as Karon's claim that 'I look in front of me and behind me and I see nothing' (p.108), Richard begins to think of the refugees not just as an academic exercise but as real, individual people. Exposed to the realities of the refugee situation, Richard's views on life begin to change and he wonders 'how many times ... must a person relearn everything he knows' (p.142) before he is able to grasp the truth of things.

Ultimately, Richard comes to understand that the meaning of life is not to be found in his ancient texts or the meandering thoughts of his past, but in connecting with people like the refugees. He experiences a profound moment of realisation during the refugees' protest at their eviction from Spandau, recognising that all life is essentially the same: fleeting, but nonetheless valuable. He notes:

> Perhaps on this level of the universe, there is no such thing as difference, there are no two halves – it's just a matter of a few pigments in the material that's known as skin in all the languages of the world ... Whether you clothe your body in hand-me-down pants and jackets from a donation bin, brand-name sweaters, expensive or cheap dresses, or uniforms with a helmet and visor – underneath this clothing, every one of us is naked and must surely, let's hope, have taken pleasure in sunshine and wind, in water and snow, have eaten or drunk this and that tasty thing, perhaps even have loved someone and been loved in return before dying one day. (p.210)

Richard's relationship with the refugees shakes him out of a self-centred world view in which his purpose was defined by his academic life and interests. He becomes aware that we are connected to the lives of those around us, even those from faraway countries and different social, religious and cultural backgrounds. He learns that, in the brief time we are on this earth, we are all the same.

Freedom and confinement

Key quotes

'[Richard would] still be trapped in his cage of free agency, imprisoned by the luxury of free choice.' (p.19)

'To investigate how one makes the transition from a full, readily comprehensible existence to the life of a refugee, which is open in all directions ... he has to know what was at the beginning, what was in the middle, and what is now.' (p.39)

'When you become foreign, Awad says, you don't have a choice.' (p.67)

'Richard thinks that he's heard the word *freedom* used in Germany to mean quite different things.' (p.170)

In spite of the apparent freedom of movement the refugees have in Germany, the reality of their situation is far more complex. While the refugees are not literally at war in the European country, the laws and restrictions of asylum hem them in on all sides.

After his first encounter with the refugees – when he has walked right past the protesting men and returned home to see the hunger strike on television – Richard feels a sense of shame at enjoying his dinner while the refugees go hungry. However, he also acknowledges that, even if he chose to join the men on a hunger strike 'he'd still be trapped in his cage of free agency, imprisoned by the luxury of free choice' (p.19). This cage of 'free agency' Richard describes is exactly what the refugees lack. While he has the 'luxury' of being able to choose whether to eat or go without, the refugees have been forced into their situation by circumstances beyond their control. The men in Alexanderplatz use the hunger strike as a way of protesting against their greater confinement. Though they currently reside in Germany, they are in no way treated as citizens, and they lack the freedom of choice that people such as Richard take for granted. This idea of freedom of choice is reinforced later, when Richard comes to the understanding that the burden of the men's memories confines them further, while those with the freedom to choose 'get to decide which stories to hold on to' (p.67).

Inspired by his developing understanding of the refugees and his newfound academic interest in their plight, Richard decides to investigate how a person ends up as a refugee with their life 'open in all directions' (p.39). Again, this 'openness' is not freedom, but a lack of clear borders that is just as confining as a real, physical boundary. Later in the text, in conversation with Apollo, the young man uses the word 'freedom' when referring to his life in Italy before moving to Germany. He tells Richard that, because he has no family, he was free to live on the streets for six months. Richard reflects 'that he's heard the word *freedom* used in Germany to mean quite different things' (p.170).

Towards the end of the novel, Erpenbeck makes one final critical remark about the freedom of choice that people in Europe have about the refugees seeking asylum in their countries. Monica, Jörg's wife and a mouthpiece for many of the casually racist sentiments that Erpenbeck criticises throughout the novel, asks, 'What does "freedom of movement" mean if not the right to travel?' (p.197). This ironic comment on freedom, made by a woman talking about her holidays, reinforces the idea that, though the refugees travel a great distance to arrive in Germany, they are still not free.

The importance of the past

Key quotes

'There's no clear link between cause and effect, there's an indirect relationship, Richard thinks ...' (p.94)

'[W]ithout memory, man is nothing more than a bit of flesh on the planet's surface.' (p.151)

'A life in which an empty present is occupied by a memory that one cannot endure, in which the future refuses to show itself, must be extremely taxing, Richard thinks ...' (p.277)

Go, Went, Gone shows that the past can be both comforting and devastating. The refugees in the text are connected to the horrors of their past by memories they would rather bury, but they are also reliant on their memories for the sense of home and family they provide. Richard's memories, tied to the era before the fall of the Berlin wall, are often nostalgic, romanticised and perhaps unreliable, and he spends a lot of his time dwelling on the past rather than thinking about his present. His knowledge of Germany's past, of the horrors of World War II in particular, is a source of shame for him, and he deliberately hides this history from the African men.

Richard reflects that 'without memory, man is nothing more than a bit of flesh on the planet's surface' (p.151). He also believes that sometimes there is 'no clear link between cause and effect' (p.94), with his own transition after the fall of the Berlin Wall making him aware that people rarely, if ever, have control over the situations in which they find themselves. When it comes to sharing memories of his country's problematic past, he 'feels deeply ashamed' that 'less than a lifetime ago, Germany systematically murdered so many human beings' (p.119). These shared memories of the atrocities committed by his country – even though he had nothing to do with them – are powerful enough to elicit strong, complex emotions in Richard.

Those remembrances of World War II are a recurrent feature throughout *Go, Went, Gone*, as Erpenbeck forces us to consider the importance of culture and history. In a chilling moment, Richard highlights the probable public outcry at the expense of transporting the refugees, comparing it to the history of 'other transports' (p.209) – here, he is referring to the networks that ran across the country conveying hundreds of thousands to their death in concentration camps.

Ultimately, it is the horrors of the memories faced by the refugees and the lives they left behind that highlight the importance of the past. At the very end of the novel Richard reflects on the problem of memories 'one cannot endure' in a life with an 'empty present' (p.277). All of the men are haunted by their past. Even Richard, filled with regret at his wife's abortion and the subsequent breakdown of their marriage, cannot escape his past. Whether it is the shared experience of an entire country, or the personal histories of individuals, the past shapes who we are and sometimes comes to fill the entire present.

DIFFERENT INTERPRETATIONS

Different interpretations arise from different responses to a text. Over time, a text will evoke a wide range of responses from its readers, who may come from various social or cultural groups and live in very different places and historical periods. Responses by critics and reviewers can be published in newspapers, journals and books, both online and in print. They can also be expressed in discussions among readers in the media, classrooms, book groups and so on.

While there is no single correct reading or interpretation of a text, it is important to understand that an interpretation is more than a personal opinion – it is the justification of a point of view on the text. To present an interpretation of a text based on your point of view, you must use a logical argument and support it with relevant evidence from the text.

Critical viewpoints

Reviews of Jenny Erpenbeck's *Go, Went, Gone* have been overwhelmingly positive, with critics praising her empathetic and compassionate detailing of the refugees' lives while also commending the harsh criticism she levels at German and European laws and regulations.

While Erpenbeck is no stranger to positive reviews, with her novel *The End of Days* winning the Independent Foreign Fiction Prize, the critical reception to *Go, Went, Gone* is particularly focused on Erpenbeck's exploration of political issues.

Eileen Battersby, writing for *The Guardian*, notes Erpenbeck's skill for presenting the humanity of the refugee men without resorting to sentimentality:

> The book could easily have become a well-intentioned polemic, but Erpenbeck combines her philosophical intellect with hours of conversations conducted with refugees to tell a very human story about a lonely, emotionally insulated man slowly discovering there is a far wider, urgent world beyond him through his meetings with extraordinary, vividly drawn migrants, each with a story to tell. (Battersby 2017)

Later in the same review, Erpenbeck is praised for writing a 'powerful tale, delivered in a wonderfully plain, candid tone'. This candid tone, in which Erpenbeck is frank and brutally honest about the state of politics in her home country, is also a key factor in a positive review from Robert Lemon, associate professor of German at the University of Oklahoma, in *World Literature Today*. Lemon praises the 'the cold fury of [Erpenbeck's] polemic against Germany and the European Union's bureaucratic response to this humanitarian crisis' (Lemon 2017).

Lemon also focuses on another element of Erpenbeck's narrative: 'the central truth that the engagement with the Other inevitably entails a reckoning with the self'. Throughout *Go, Went, Gone*, the reader is forced to consider Richard's initial ignorance of the refugee situation, and the various reactions of his friends, as a mirror to their own thoughts and feelings. As well as criticising the bureaucracy of the crisis, Erpenbeck forces us to look inwards and to question how much attention we pay to the plight of people such as those in the novel.

The critical success of *Go, Went, Gone* extends beyond Erpenbeck herself. In 2017, translator Susan Bernofsky was awarded the English PEN Award for her translation of the novel from German to English. Clearly, the crisis facing the refugees and Erpenbeck's criticism of the European response is powerful in any language.

Two interpretations of *Go, Went, Gone*

Interpretation 1: *Go, Went, Gone* suggests that the refugee crisis is a hopeless situation.

Although Richard's attempts to help the refugees he meets are valiant, they are ultimately futile in the face of the larger humanitarian crisis that the men represent. The hopelessness of the situation faced by the African refugees is evident throughout the text, and the enormity of the situation – this is a *global* crisis, not just an African or European issue – is simply overwhelming.

Beginning with Richard's self-absorption and blindness to the protests at Alexanderplatz, Erpenbeck uses her protagonist to point out how the general populace understands the crisis. Though the men in Alexanderplatz hold a placard that reads '*We become visible*' (p.14), the truth is entirely the opposite. It is the invisibility of the men that presents one of the most hopeless aspects to the crisis, for if the men cannot be seen by those from whom they seek help, then how can they ever get the assistance they require?

Even when Richard finally notices the refugees, watching back these scenes on the evening news, he initially takes only an academic interest. Again, Richard is representative of a significant portion of the public both in Germany and beyond. We see the crisis unfolding on the news, but the bare statistics and sheer volume of people damaged by the various wars and conflicts in Africa do not connect emotionally. Without an emotional, personal connection to the refugees, we are as cold and distant as Richard, simply analysing the situation without really connecting with the people involved.

Erpenbeck uses the relationship between Richard and the refugees, formed throughout his interviews, to build this empathetic connection; yet it is still not enough to solve any of the real issues faced by the refugees. Richard's interviews quickly make him realise that the horrors faced by these men exceed the statistics and emotionless reporting seen on the news. He learns that they are real individuals, humans just like him, and that the horrific things that have happened in their past are only being exacerbated by their current situation in Germany. Yet even with this knowledge, and the elevated status afforded to him as a European citizen, there is little Richard can do to help the men. Richard knows that 'the refugees can't afford a lawyer, and they barely understand German' (p.104). He attempts to navigate the complex laws and regulations, such as 'Dublin II', that govern the men's lives, but the 'iron law' (p.180) is a beast that devours everyone before it without emotion. Richard is helpless when the men are evicted from Spandau and most of them have their applications for asylum revoked. While he is able to offer brief comfort to some of the men, such as buying land for Karon's family and offering Rufu and others a floor to sleep on after their evictions, his gestures are short-lived and do not address the greater problems.

A sense of hopelessness extends from the past, through the present, and into the future. Richard reflects that, for the refugees, 'an empty present is occupied by a memory that one cannot endure' (p.277), and Karon tells Richard, 'I look in front of me and behind me and I see nothing' (p.108). It is little wonder that, at one point, Richard feels as though he has 'truly relinquished all hope' (p.175). Though he is able to play a small part in making the lives of individual refugees better, the sheer scale of the crisis means that, ultimately, the situation is without hope.

Interpretation 2: *Go, Went, Gone* suggests that hope comes in the form of small acts of kindness.

Although the enormity of the refugees' legal situation might suggest a level of hopelessness, the small acts of kindness shown by Richard and some of his friends indicate that there is a real possibility for positive change.

Firstly, the fact that Richard evolves throughout the text from a self-absorbed and oblivious academic to an empathetic activist proves that there is hope. Richard represents aspects of Erpenbeck's readership, both in his initial ambivalence towards the crisis and in his distance from the men when he begins the interviews. Though he begins his interviews by cataloguing the men's interests and backgrounds and asking questions that do not truly probe the deeper meanings of their flight from Africa, he quickly finds that he is unable to maintain an academic distance. The men's stories affect Richard – and the reader – on a deep and personal level. Erpenbeck demonstrates that if there is hope for a man such as Richard to become more empathetic, then there is hope for all of us, as long as we are willing to go beyond the cold statistics of the situation and explore the effects on individual human lives.

The refugees themselves frequently appear to be without hope. Karon's comment that he 'see[s] nothing' (p.108) when he pictures the future is echoed in Rashid's sense of despair at being unable to work and Osarobo's fears that all Europeans believe black men are criminals. The men have experienced terrible hardships not only in Africa and during the journey to Europe, but also in Italy and Germany. However, they are also capable of experiencing moments that suggest that all hope is not lost: Osarobo connects with Richard on a personal level while learning to play the piano at his home; Rashid uses his relationship with Richard to help unburden himself of some of the horrific memories of his past; Rufu is encouraged by Richard to stop the medication that is making him sick; and several of the men are offered a place to stay, by Richard and his friends, when they are evicted from Spandau.

Richard's small acts of kindness towards the men even extend to helping them financially. While it cannot be argued that Richard purchasing land for Karon's family solves the greater crisis, or addresses the reason Karon fled Africa in the first place, t at least offers a glimmer of hope to one family. Richard feels incapable of helping all of the men and realises the enormity of the legal situation and his inability to address it. In his despair Richard decides to assist at least one of the men, but for Karon, the individual whose family can now envisage a future, the gesture is not a small one. Erpenbeck suggests that in these acts of kindness is a greater message: if we all acted like Richard and took care of the few people around us, then perhaps the greater benefit would follow.

QUESTIONS & ANSWERS

This section focuses on your own analytical writing on the text, and gives you strategies for producing high-quality responses in your coursework and exam essays.

Essay writing – an overview

An essay on a literary work is a formal and serious piece of writing that presents your point of view on the text, usually in response to a given topic. Your 'point of view' in an essay is your interpretation of the meaning of the text's language, structure, characters, situations and events, supported by detailed analysis of textual evidence.

Analyse – don't summarise

In your essays it is important to avoid simply summarising what happens in a text.

- A **summary** is a description or paraphrase (retelling in different words) of the characters and events. For example: 'Macbeth has a horrifying vision of a dagger dripping with blood before he goes to murder King Duncan.'
- An **analysis** is an explanation of the real meaning or significance that lies 'beneath' the text's words (and images, for a film). For example: 'Macbeth's vision of a bloody dagger shows how deeply uneasy he is about the violent act he is contemplating, and conveys his sense that supernatural forces are impelling him to act.'

A limited amount of summary is sometimes necessary to let your reader know which part of the text you wish to discuss. However, always keep this to a minimum and follow it immediately with your analysis of what this part of the text is really telling us.

Plan your essay

Carefully plan your essay so that you have a clear idea of what you are going to say. The plan ensures that your ideas flow logically, that your argument remains consistent and that you stay on the topic. An essay plan should be a list of **brief dot points** covering no more than half a page.

- Include your central argument or main contention – a concise statement of your overall response to the topic.
- Write three or four dot points for each paragraph, indicating the main idea and evidence/examples from the text. Note that in your essay you will need to expand on these points and analyse the evidence.

Structure your essay

An essay is a complete, self-contained piece of writing. It has a clear beginning (the introduction), middle (several body paragraphs) and end (the last paragraph or conclusion). It must also have a central argument that runs throughout, linking each paragraph to form a coherent whole. See examples of introductions and conclusions in the 'Analysing a sample topic' and 'Sample answer' sections.

The introduction establishes your overall response to the topic. It includes your main contention and outlines the main evidence you will refer to in the course of the essay. Write your introduction after you have done a plan and before you write the rest of the essay.

The body paragraphs argue your case – they present evidence from the text and explain how this evidence supports your argument. Each body paragraph needs:

- a strong **topic sentence** (usually the first sentence) that states the main point being made in the paragraph
- **evidence** from the text, including some brief quotations
- **analysis** of the textual evidence, with **explanation** of its significance and how it supports your argument
- **links back to the topic** in one or more statements, usually towards the end of the paragraph.

Connect the body paragraphs so that your discussion flows smoothly. Use some linking words and phrases such as 'similarly' and 'on the other hand', though don't start every paragraph like this. Another strategy is to use a significant word from the last sentence of one paragraph in the first sentence of the next.

Use key terms from the topic – or synonyms for them – throughout, so the relevance of your discussion to the topic is always clear.

The conclusion ties everything together and finishes the essay. It includes strong statements that emphasise your central argument and provide a clear response to the topic.

Avoid simply restating the points made earlier in the essay – this will end on a very flat note and imply that you have run out of ideas and vocabulary. The conclusion should be a logical extension of what you have written, not just a repetition or summary of it. Writing an effective conclusion can be a challenge. Try using these tips:

- Start by linking back to the final sentence of the second-last paragraph, rather than leaping to your main contention straight away – this helps your writing to flow.
- Use synonyms and expressions with equivalent meanings to vary your vocabulary. This allows you to reinforce your line of argument without being repetitive.
- When planning your essay, think of one or two broad statements or observations about the text's wider meaning. These should be related to the topic and your overall argument. Keep them for the conclusion, since they will give you something 'new' to say but still follow logically from your discussion. The introduction will be focused on the topic, but the conclusion can present a wider view of the text.

Essay topics

1. 'Go, Went, Gone shows how an individual can make a difference in the world.' Discuss.
2. 'Understanding the past is vital in helping us to understand ourselves.'
   Discuss the importance of the past in *Go, Went, Gone*.
3. 'Richard is never truly able to understand the troubles the refugees face.'
   To what extent do you agree?
4. "I look in front of me and behind me and I see nothing."
   '*Go, Went, Gone* is a novel without hope.' Do you agree?
5. 'Richard uses literature to escape the reality of what is happening in the world around him.' Discuss.
6. 'The characters in *Go, Went, Gone* are unable to escape their past.' Discuss.
7. How does Erpenbeck highlight the flaws in German and European laws in *Go, Went, Gone*?
8. "But the problem is very big, it has a wife and many, many children."
   How does Erpenbeck demonstrate the scale of the refugee crisis?
9. What role does language play in *Go, Went, Gone*?
10. How does Erpenbeck demonstrate the importance of changing perspectives in *Go, Went, Gone*?

Vocabulary for writing on *Go, Went, Gone*

Allusion: An indirect reference to something, such as another text.

Asylum seeker: A person who has left their home country as a refugee and is legally seeking asylum in another country.

Dublin II: A regulation that states that only one EU member state or country can be responsible for a refugee's legal status.

Economic expediency: Prioritising financial considerations over human wellbeing.

Existential: Relating to a philosophy that explores the meaning of life and free will.

Gaddafi: Libyan head of state from 1969 to 2011 who was accused of supporting international terrorism and ultimately overthrown in 2011 following a civil uprising.

Intertextuality: Connection between one text and another, such as allusions or direct references to other texts – for example, the intertextual reference to Greek myth in Richard's naming of Apollo.

Motif: A recurring symbol in a text, such as the man in the lake.

Persecution: Hostility and prejudice against a person or group, often based on ethnicity or religion.

Philology: A branch of study concerned with the history and development of languages and texts.

Poignant: Evoking a sense of sadness, regret or nostalgia.

Refugee: A person who is forced to leave their home as a result of politics, war or natural disaster.

Totensonntag*:* A German Protestant holiday that commemorates the dead.

Analysing a sample topic

"But the problem is very big, it has a wife and many, many children." How does Erpenbeck demonstrate the scale of the refugee crisis?

This topic requires you to grapple with the complexities of the refugee crisis, as presented by Erpenbeck through her various characters. The quotation – from one of the refugees, Karon – represents the enormity of the situation. In order to present a well-rounded argument, you must address multiple aspects of the refugee crisis.

'How' questions also require some acknowledgment of the language, structure and techniques used by the author – that is, the construction of the text. For example, you could discuss the use of fiction to explore a real-world problem, or the unusual language features and structures Erpenbeck uses to include distinct points of view in her narrative.

Sample introduction

> *Go, Went, Gone* presents a complex perspective on the refugee crisis through the interwoven narratives of the refugees' lives. Through the central perspective of Richard – a retired professor who is initially naive about the refugee crisis – Erpenbeck reveals the lives and trials of a number of men from unique but equally troubled backgrounds. Erpenbeck's narrative weaves between Richard's interviews, the men's memories and critical opinions on real-world laws and regulations to create a compelling story that explores the enormity of the refugee crisis.

Body paragraph outline

Paragraph 1: Describe how Richard's interviews provide the most information on the refugee crisis.

- Richard, like the general reader, begins the story with little understanding of the scale of the refugee crisis.
- He initially takes an academic, distant interest in the crisis.
- Through Richard's interviews, Erpenbeck reveals the human side of the crisis.
- As the narrative progresses, Richard's – and therefore the reader's – understanding of the complexities of the refugee crisis grows.

Paragraph 2: Discuss techniques Erpenbeck uses to present other perspectives.

- Erpenbeck occasionally switches perspective, such as moving into the thoughts of Apollo or Tristan/Awad.

- Richard's circle of friends presents the varied views of German society on the refugee crisis.
- Snapshots of the memories of the refugee men, such as Rashid's heartbreaking story of the death of his children at sea, provide the most compelling perspective on the refugee crisis.

Paragraph 3: Explore the various real-world laws and regulations being criticised in Erpenbeck's novel.

- Given the complexity of the laws and regulations surrounding asylum seeking in Europe, Richard's ignorance is understandable. Like the reader, he is initially naive, but he makes an effort to study the laws, thus developing his perspective on the issue.
- A discussion of one particular piece of legislation – Dublin II – demonstrates Erpenbeck's point that the laws surrounding asylum are almost designed to confuse and complicate an already complex issue.
- Richard's visit to the lawyer, who expresses a genteel but resigned attitude, shows that even those with the potential to do something are powerless in the face of the law.

Sample conclusion

> Through the complex interwoven narratives of the refugee men, and Richard's growing understanding of their problems, Erpenbeck reveals the enormity of the refugee crisis. Fleeing war and persecution in Africa, the men find themselves in precarious situations when they reach the supposed safety of Europe. Through stories of horrific trials, such as Rashid and Tristan's journeys from Africa, to the ongoing racism and persecution faced by men like Apollo and Osarobo, the men's stories reveal that the refugee crisis extends beyond Africa. As Richard continues his interviews, the reader is forced to accept the reality of a situation in which faceless and emotionless laws affect the lives of real, individual humans. Ultimately, Erpenbeck challenges a system that not only ignores the scale of the refugee crisis, but actually makes it worse.

SAMPLE ANSWER

'Understanding the past is vital in helping us to understand ourselves.' Discuss the importance of the past in *Go, Went, Gone*.

While the past can be a place of refuge, it can also be a source of pain. In *Go, Went, Gone*, the characters grapple with the horrors of their past lives and come to terms with the present. As Richard interviews the refugee men, he not only learns of their past and the present situations they find themselves in, but also faces some of the darkness in his own past. The refugees themselves reveal both the pain and the love in their past lives, in stories that range from terrifying to heartbreaking. In exploring their memories and the journeys they have taken thus far, Richard and the refugees learn to accept the present.

Richard begins his interviews purely as an academic exercise, but as soon as he begins to understand the refugees' histories, he is forced to confront issues in the present. Initially, Richard does not even notice the men. He walks by them in Alexanderplatz and 'doesn't hear' the protests they are making about their present situation. However, once he connects with the refugees through his interviews, he quickly comes to understand that a series of terrible events in the past led them to where they are now. Richard – a retired professor of classics – feels he is well versed in understanding history. But his understanding of the men's past is limited, and only informed by out-of-date literature such as his never-used copy of *Negerliteratur* and a vague knowledge of the countries in Africa. Once he begins his interviews, however, he learns of the horrors in recent history, from Apollo's so-called family who 'tried to beat him to death' to Awad's story of the night his father died. Richard quickly begins to understand that the men's current lives – stranded in Germany and caught between legal loopholes – are almost as challenging as their past lives.

For Richard, the interviews also force him to focus on aspects of his own past and learn to accept his current position in life. At the beginning of the novel, Richard finds himself at a loose end – recently retired and at a loss as to how to spend his time. He wanders his house trapped in memories of his own past, particularly his relationships with his wife and his former lover. As he begins his interviews, however, he starts to make comparisons between the men's lives and his own. He reflects on his youth behind the Berlin Wall in East Berlin and on the arbitrary nature of borders that divide people. Just like the borders and violence that define the lives of the refugees, Richard acknowledges that there is 'no clear link between cause and effect': the refugees have just as little control over their lives as Richard had over his when the wall came down. Borders – like the one separating East Germany from West Germany in Richard's past, or Africa from Europe in the refugee men's present – only exist on maps and in laws. In reality, Richard realises, people are all alike. Richard acknowledges that, despite the horrors in the men's past lives and the relative calm of his own, they all share experiences of love and loss that unite them in the present as human beings.

The most important aspect of the past is the memories we hold on to, and how they shape us in the present. Richard shies away from his own memories, denying to himself until the very last minute the harm he caused his wife. Through the relationship with the refugees, however, and the shared knowledge of their struggles, Richard is finally able to admit to himself and his friends some of the shame he felt over his wife's abortion. Similarly, he is ashamed of some of his past thoughts, such as the 'tiny corner of his soul' that hoped that Africans 'mourn their dead less', or even the collective shame of the horrors of World War II. Richard's relationship with the refugees enables him to grapple with and accept responsibility for some of this shame. The refugees themselves must also face up to their memories. While some, like Karon and Osarobo, are initially vague or evasive, many of the refugees open up to Richard and share their memories with him. He understands the necessity of memories, and that without them we are 'nothing more than a bit of flesh'. In his own, small way, Richard helps the refugees come to terms with memories they 'cannot endure', helping them to accept their 'empty present'. Through the sharing of memories, Richard and the refugees help each other to better understand and cope with the situation in which they find themselves.

Ultimately, the relationship between the refugees and Richard is mutually beneficial. As Richard interviews the men and learns of their past lives, he sees reflections in his own life that help him to come to terms with some of the shame and disappointment in his own history. The refugees unburden themselves of some of their horrific memories, using Richard as a sounding board for some of the darkness in their past. It is through these characters and their interactions with one another that Erpenbeck reveals why understanding the past is crucial if we are to understand ourselves.

REFERENCES & READING

The text

Erpenbeck, J 2018, *Go, Went, Gone,* trans. S Bernofsky, Portobello Books, London.

Other sources

Amnesty International 2020, 'Libya: New evidence shows refugees and migrants trapped in horrific cycle of abuses', 24 September, https://www.amnesty.org/en/latest/news/2020/09/libya-new-evidence-shows-refugees-and-migrants-trapped-in-horrific-cycle-of-abuses/

Battersby, E 2017, '*Go, Went, Gone* by Jenny Erpenbeck review – humanising migration', *The Guardian*, 23 September, https://www.theguardian.com/books/2017/sep/23/go-went-gone-review-jenny-erpenbeck

Lemon, R 2017, '*Go, Went, Gone* by Jenny Erpenbeck', September, https://www.worldliteraturetoday.org/2017/september/go-went-gone-jenny-erpenbeck

McHugh-Dillon, R 2018, 'The lives of others: A review of Jenny Erpenbeck's *Go, Went, Gone*', *The Lifted Brow*, 7 December, https://www.theliftedbrow.com/liftedbrow/2018/12/7/the-lives-of-others-a-review-of-jenny-erpenbecks-go-went-gone-by-ruth-mchugh-dillon

Messud, C 2017, 'Lives other than his own', *The New York Times*, 12 December, https://www.nytimes.com/2017/12/12/books/review/go-went-gone-jenny-erpenbeck.html

Oltermann, P 2020, 'Jenny Erpenbeck: "My experience of East Germany is changed by every book I read"', *The Guardian*, 12 December https://www.theguardian.com/books/2020/dec/12/jenny-erpenbeck-my-experience-of-east-germany-is-changed-by-every-book-i-read

UNHCR 2008, 'The Dublin Regulation', https://www.unhcr.org/4a9d13d59.pdf

UNHCR 2017, 'Libya: QIPs', 23 October, https://www.unhcr.org/en-au/libya.html

UNHCR 2019, 'Libya-Niger situation', 12 November, https://reliefweb.int/sites/reliefweb.int/files/resources/72298.pdf

Wood, J 2017, 'A novelist's powerful response to the refugee crisis', *The New Yorker*, 18 September, https://www.newyorker.com/magazine/2017/09/25/a-novelists-powerful-response-to-the-refugee-crisis